Platform Phonics 2

Helen Craddock

Leopard Learning

Find out more about our books!

Leopard Learning

If you would like to find out more about our books, simply complete and return this photocopiable form with a large stamped addressed envelope

Name _____

Address _____

_____ Postcode _____

Please return to: *Leopard Learning*, PO Box 2271, BA2 6YZ

Don't forget the large stamped addressed envelope!

Text © Helen Craddock 1999
Illustrations © Leopard Learning 1999
First published by Leopard Learning Ltd, PO Box 2271, Bath, BA2 6YZ

The right of Helen Craddock to be identified as the author of this work has been asserted by her in accordance with the Copyright, Designs and Patents Act 1988.

The copyright holders authorise ONLY users of Platform Phonics 2 to make photocopies or stencil duplicates of the copymasters for their own or their classes' immediate use within the teaching context.

No other rights are granted without permission in writing from the publishers or under license from the Copyright Licensing Agency Limited. Further details of such licenses (for reprographic reproduction) may be obtained from the Copyright Licensing Agency Limited, 90 Tottenham Court Road, London W1P 9HE.

Copy by any other means or for any other purpose is strictly prohibited without the prior written consent of the copyright holders. Applications for such permission should be addressed to the publishers.

A catalogue record for this book is available from the British Library.

ISBN 1 8999 29 45 2

Typeset by Leopard Learning Ltd, Bath

Printed in Great Britain by Redwood Books Ltd. Trowbridge

Contents

What is Platform Phonics?	1
What this book covers	1
How this book is organised	2
Teaching blending skills	3
Teaching the high frequency words	3
Using Platform Phonics in the literacy hour	4
Ideas for working through the literacy hour with this book	6
Using the units and the general copymasters	8

The copymasters

Unit 1: sp -sp st -st sk -sk	1-7
Unit 2: th thr -th ch -tch sh -sh	8-15
Unit 3: sc scr sm sn squ sw	16-21
Unit 4: bl cl fl gl pl sl	22-28
Unit 5: br cr dr fr gr pr str tr	29-36
Unit 6: -ld -lf -lk -lp -lt -ct -xt -xty -ft -pt -nt	37-43
Unit 7: -mp -nd -ng -nk et en in on al el il ol	44-51
Unit 8: -dd -ff -gg -ll -mm -nn -nn -tt -ss -zz	52-56
Unit 9: a-e i-e o-e u-e	57-61
Unit 10: ai ay oi oy ee ea all	62-69
Unit 11: oo oo oa ou aw ew ow	70-77
Unit 12: ar are air er ear eer	78-84
Unit 13: ir ire or ore ur ure	85-91
General copymasters	92-99

What is Platform Phonics?

Platform Phonics is a complete structured photocopiable resource for teaching essential phonic skills at Key Stage 1 and at P1 to P3 in Scotland.

It aims to develop phonological awareness, phonic knowledge, word recognition and sound symbol relationship - all the skills that the National Literacy Strategy defines as being word level. The National Literacy Strategy states that 'At Key Stage 1, there should be a strong emphasis on the teaching of phonics and other word level skills.
Pupils should be taught to:
- Discriminate between the separate sounds in words;
- Learn the letters and letter combinations most commonly used to spell those sounds;
- Read words by sounding out and blending their separate parts;
- Write words by combining the spelling patterns of their sounds.'

Platform Phonics 1 and *2* cover all these skills.

Platform Phonics teaches children the relationship of the sound of a letter with its written symbol and how to build letters into words as soon as the first two letters are learnt. The two books cover the single letter sounds, consonant blends and digraphs, and the most commonly used vowel blends and digraphs. The rules are taught through a structured programme that builds up from unit to unit, although teachers can also draw on the materials more flexibly to meet their needs. The high frequency words listed in the National Literacy Strategy for Reception classes and Years 1 and 2 are all covered through word building activities or by learning them as sight or 'star' words.

Through copymasters and a series of suggested games and activities *Platform Phonics* ensures that by the time children have completed these books they have a thorough grounding in phonics and related work attack skills. You will find that, not only are these books of real, practical value but that they can be used successfully alongside the reading scheme or reading programme being used in your school, and within the structure of the Literacy Hour, for both younger children and older special needs pupils. By the end of *Platform Phonics 1* alone, children will be able to read 800 words by blending as well as nearly fifty sight words through the built-in sight words on the copymasters.

These books contain all the key features of other books in Leopard Learning's *Platform* range:
- Carefully structured progression which is broken down into very small steps so that there are no big leaps in learning.
- Lots of practice at each step.
- A large bank of highly motivational and worthwhile copymasters. Each sheet provides considerable practice and value to make your journey to the photocopier worthwhile and cost-effective.
- Carefully worded instructions that use a low reading age and frequently repeated patterns of activities and allow children to work as independently as possible.
- Regular checks on learning through the Learning Maps at the end of every unit.

What this book covers

Platform Phonics 2 builds on the work of *Platform Phonics 1*, teaching the skills children need to develop further their phonological awareness (the ability to detect sounds within words) and phonic skills through a structured programme. It introduces children to the necessary facts, conventions and skills of phonics which are essential to becoming a fluent reader and provides a firm foundation for reading, writing and spelling.

It covers:
- Initial blends such as 'sp', 'bl' and 'cr'
- Final blends such as '-st' and '-lp'.
- the use of 'magic' or marker 'e': 'a-e', 'i-e' etc.
- Long vowels and diphthongs, for example: 'ai', 'ee' etc.
- vowels with 'r': 'ar', 'ear' etc.
- learning to blend these sounds together to make words.
- continuing on from *Platform Phonics 1*, the remainder of the high-frequency word listed in the National Literacy Strategy which children need to recognise by sight by the end of Year 2. These are taught either through phonic building activities or as sight or 'Star' words.
- learning to spell through the look, visualise, write and check method.

In this book, consonant strings are taught before vowel combinations because they give more insight into word recognition than vowels. They are constant in over 90% of cases and provide the developing reader with much more effective clues to meaning than vowels. For example, 'J_ck _nd J_ll w_nt _p th_ h_ll t_ f_tch _ p_ _l _f w_t_r' is comprehensible without its vowels. It is not until consonants are established that most of the various vowel blends and digraphs are introduced.

The teaching of high frequency words is built into the book in two ways:
- words which are phonically regular are introduced through blending activities as the sounds are introduced.
- irregular words which do not conform to regular spelling patterns and which have to be learned by sight are introduced gradually throughout the book by means of a special feature: Star Words, which is explained below.

Platform Phonics presents phonics in a systematic way. Through a structured programme it teaches children the skills they need to develop phonological awareness (the ability to detect sounds within words) and to blend sounds to make words. Research has established that children's ability to discern and manipulate the sounds which make up spoken words is strongly linked with their ability to read.

Working in units helps children to analyse the effect of blending different letters with one other e.g. s + various consonants (Unit 3). Some children will only need to dip into areas where they are weak whilst others will need to cover all the units. There is no right or wrong way to work through this book. You should feel free to use it according to the needs of the children in your class.

How this book is organised

Platform Phonics 2 consists of 13 structured units of work, preceeded by this introductory material. For each unit there are general instructions, which are found at the front of the book on pages 8-10, and a suite of photocopiable materials. At the back of the book there is a section of general copymasters which provides you with flashcards, alphabet cards and record sheets.

Phonic order

In *Platform Phonics 2* letter strings are not taught alphabetically but grouped in units which enable children to create a structure in their minds and so learn the phonic rules more easily. The letter strings are taught in the following order:

Unit 1	consonants	sp, -sp, st,-st, sk, -sk;
Unit 2	consonant digraphs	th, thr, -th, ch, -tch, sh -sh;
Unit 3	's' plus a consonant	sc, scr, sm, sn, squ, sw;
Unit 4	consonant plus 'l'	bl, cl, fl, gl, pl, sl;
Unit 5	consonant plus 'r'	br, cr, dr, fr, gr, pr, tr;
Unit 6	'l' plus final consonants	-ld, -lf, -lk, -lp, -lt;
	't' plus final consonants	-ct, -ft, -nt, -pt, -xt;
Unit 7	other blends and digraphs	-mp, -nd, -ng, -nk, et, en, in, on, al, el, il, ol;
Unit 8	double consonants	-dd, -ff, -gg, -ll, -mm, -nn, -ss, -tt, -zz;
Unit 9	marker 'e'	a-e, i-e-, o-e, u-e;
Unit 10	long vowels	ai, ay, oi, oy, ee, ea, all;
Unit 11	long vowels	oo, oo, oa, ou, aw, ew, ow;
Unit 12	extended vowels	ar, are, air, er, ear, eer;
Unit 13	extended vowels	ir, ire, or, ore, ur, ure

The units

You will find instructions for using the units on pages 8-10. Each unit provides a structured sequence of copymasters which each introduce one sound. The unit ends with a Learning Map. This is an assessment page which consolidates the work of the unit. It will provide you, the teacher, with a record of progress made to date and will confirm for the child what he or she knows. You will find that the units cover a range of activities which will reinforce the sound being learned in different ways. There is, however, careful patterning of the activities and instructions, so that once children have got used to the format of the sheets they can largely work on their own. This is particularly valuable during the group and independent section of the Literacy Hour when classroom management is often an important issue for the busy infant teacher.

The key feature of the units in *Platform Phonics* is that they are carefully structured. Each one uses only sounds already taught to make and blend words. These build up from unit to unit so that children are not presented with sounds they have not covered. Children can confidently use all the letter strings and combinations they meet to read and write words. (See the advice on teaching blending skills on page 3 for more on this.)

The copymasters

Each sheet introduces a new letter string combination within a unit. As well as learning to write and say the sound a range of other blending and writing activities are introduced.

Usually each pair of sheets teach one Star Word - this is a high frequency word which can only be learned by sight, as it is phonically irregular. You will find these in star shaped frames, usually towards the bottom of the pages. You can use these in many different ways. For example children can cut them out and collect them in the special fold-up booklet on the last page of this book or colour them in when they know them. (See the general advice on teaching the high frequency

words below.) Alternatively you can ignore the star words altogether if they do not serve your purpose, or photocopy from a master which has them blanked out. The star words are also revisited at the end of the unit in the learning maps.
You will find more detailed advice on using the sheets on pages 8-10.

General copymasters
At the back of the book from Copymaster 92 on, there are general copymasters which provide support materials for games and activities. These include:
- flashcards of the high frequency words all children need to know
- alphabet cards
- a high frequency words check list
- a star words fold-up word book

Teaching blending skills

Platform Phonics 2 continues the work on blending started in *Platform Phonics 1*. It begins with consonant strings then moves on to the more complex vowel sounds. Research studies indicate that young children find it relatively easy to detect syllables in spoken words, to hear the beginning (onset) and vowel and letter string endings (rime) but find it quite difficult to identify the constituent phonemes of which the word is made. 'Onset' refers to the initial consonant(s) at the beginning of each syllable e.g. *bl*ackboard, *st*ockroom, *scr*atch. 'Rime' refers to a vowel and its following consonants at the end of a word e.g. w*itch*, st*itch*, d*itch*; cl*ump*, st*ump*, d*ump*. The work in *Platform Phonics 2* helps children to identify onset and rime as well as the phonemic elements of words.

Activities that develop the concept of blending
Here are a few activities to help with blending. Others are found in 'Ideas for working through the Literacy Hour' on page 6.
- Onset: say at least two consonants to form the beginning of a word and then ask children to give you a word which begins with that sound.
- Rime: ask children to clearly identify rimes. Which one of these is different and why: 'fair', 'pair', 'hear' and 'hair'?
- Onset and rime: show two letter cards which blend to make an ending e.g. 'ip' then show letter strings they already know which could begin the word such as 'ch' or 'sh'. As children become more proficient put up some letters which will not make a proper word when added to the rime e.g. 'th -ip'.
- What sounds can they hear in the middle of words such as 'toot', 'tart', 'tote'?
- What word can they hear inside words such as 'crate', 'mate', 'plate', 'skate'?
- Onset: play 'I Spy' using single, double or even treble consonants e.g. s/st/str.

While working through *Platform Phonics 1* children learnt to blend letters to form over eight hundred words. They also learned eighty-four high frequency words and to build parts of many more. By the end of this book children will be able to build thousands of words and know all the essential high frequency words on the National Strategy lists for Reception and Years 1 and 2. This will give children a firm foundation in phonic skills which puts them well on the road to becoming fluent readers.

Teaching the high frequency words

This book builds on the work on learning high frequency words started in *Platform Phonics 1*. *Platform Phonics 1* covered all 45 words for the Reception year plus 49 Year 1 and 2 words. By the end of this second book children will have learnt all the rest of the words from List 1 of the National Literacy Strategy (pages 60 and 61) for Reception and Years 1 and 2 plus the primary and secondary colours and cardinal numbers from one to ten.

The phonically regular words on this list can be built up through the work of the units but those which cannot be built are taught as Star words.

The alphabetic order for the new high frequency words from List 1 learned in this book is as follows (the star words are in italics):
about, after, again, *another*, back, ball, *because*, been, boy, *brother*, call(ed), came, *can't*, could, do, don't, door, first, girl, good, *half*, home, *house*, how, *last, laugh, little, live(d), love*, made, make, *many*, may, more, much, name, new, next, night, now, off, *old*, once, or, *our*, over, *people*, pull, *push*, saw, *school*, seen, *should*, sister, take, than, that, *their*, them, then, *these*, time, too, took, tree, *want, water*, way, *were*, *what*, *when*, where, who, will, *would*, *your*.

In addition the following numbers and colours are added as star words: *eight, four, blue, orange, white, yellow*. These added to numbers already covered in *Platform Phonics 1* and colours and numbers which can be built phonically comprise the complete set. In addition *own* is used as a star word to introduce the sound 'ow' as in mow, row, show.

You will find all core high frequency words on page 61 of the National Literacy Strategy included as small copiable flashcards on Copymasters 92-95. Children are encouraged to write as well as read the irregular high frequency words by using the Look, Visualise, Write and Check routine. Look, Visualise, Write and Check is a simple but effective technique for learning spellings. To use the technique children should:

1. Study the word noting features such as: visual shape (the number of ascenders and descenders); whether there is another word hidden inside it; whether letters are repeated etc.
2. Close their eyes and see the word 'behind the eyelids' so imprinting it on their short term memory.
3. Trace the word with their finger with their eyes still closed.
4. Open their eyes, cover the word and write it from memory.
5. Check the word. If it is mis-spelt, tick the letters that are correct and analyse why others were wrong.
6. If there are mistakes do the Look, Visualise, Write and Check stages again. If the word is correctly spelt, ask the child to write it three times from memory as quickly as they can.

Make flash cards of these high frequency words using Copymasters 92-95 and take advantage of every possible situation to help children develop an automatic response to them. There are many opportunities to collect and display words in the classroom; for example plant a branching twig in a bucket of earth or sand and label the bucket 'Words we know'. Hang cards on it which feature the ten most recently learnt sight words or those which children have found particularly difficult. The words could be hung in the shape of stars. (The learning maps provide extra practice in learning sight words.)

Using Platform Phonics in the literacy hour

The National Literacy Strategy states that 'Literacy is at the heart of the drive to raise standards in schools'. Part of being literate means that pupils should:
- 'read and write with confidence, fluency and understanding;
- be able to orchestrate a full range of reading cues (phonic, graphic, syntactic, contextual) to monitor their reading and correct their own mistakes;

- understand the sound and spelling system and use this to read and spell accurately;
- have fluent and legible handwriting;
- have an interest in words and their meanings and a growing vocabulary.'

The structure of the framework for teaching literacy is conceived at three levels: word level, sentence level and text level. *Platform Phonics* focuses on the first of these, word level, which includes phonological awareness, phonics, spelling, word recognition, graphic knowledge, vocabulary extension and handwriting.

The document stresses that, from the outset, pupils should be taught to use the word level strategies of phonic sounds and spelling and to differentiate between the different sounds of letters and letter combinations that make up a word. Children need to be able to use their knowledge of sounds and spellings in order to decode individual words and so obtain meaning from more challenging texts. The National Literacy Strategy document states that 'It is essential that pupils are taught basic decoding and spelling skills from the outset', and that 'At Key Stage 1, there should be a strong and systematic emphasis on the teaching of phonics and other word level skills'. It goes on to say that 'Pupils should be taught to:
- discriminate between the separate sounds in words;
- learn the letters and letter combinations most commonly used to spell those sounds;
- read words by sounding out and blending their separate parts;
- write words by combining the spelling patterns of their sounds.'

Platform Phonics has been written to fill this need. Phonics, spelling and correct letter formation are taught in an integrated manner and children are encouraged to form and write words as soon as they know the first two letters – first with the class as a whole then within a small group and as individuals.

The literacy clock diagram on the next page gives an overview of how *Platform Phonics* can be successfully used within the hour. The core resource of the book, the copymasters, will largely be used within the group and independent work section, but the underlying strategies can be adopted across the whole hour.

The work of *Platform Phonics* has been designed to fit the structure recommended for the Literacy

Using Platform Phonics in the literacy hour

4
- Review, discuss, assess and reflect on day's work.
- Revise new information, consolidate and clarify any misconceptions in day's lesson.
- Re-emphasise today's teaching points.

1
- Share reading of text.
- Focus on:
    recognition of known words
    word building from known letters
    spelling patterns in the story - e.g. cat, sat, mat
    word order in the sentences.
- Create text with known words or words that can be built from known letters.

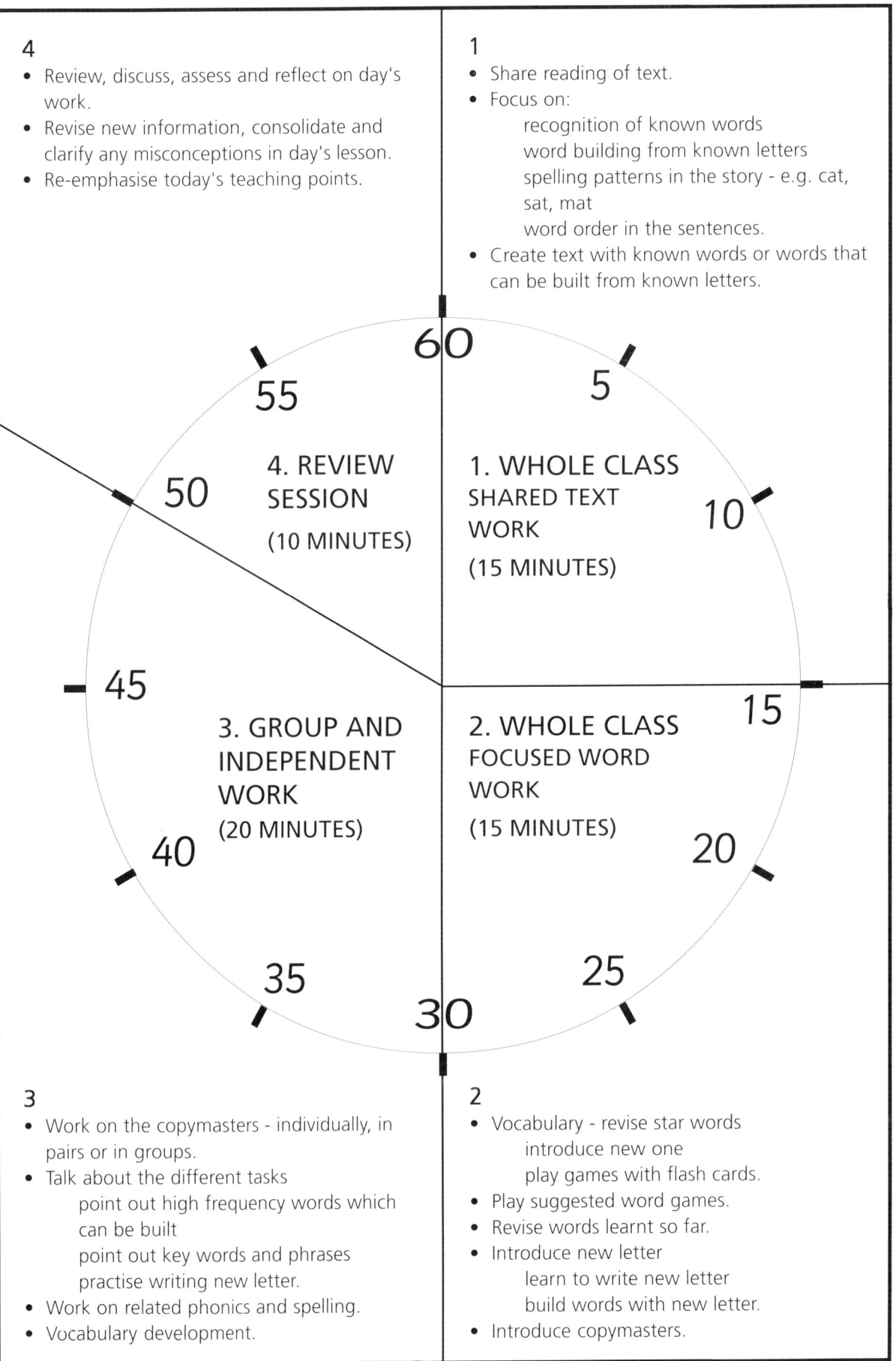

3
- Work on the copymasters - individually, in pairs or in groups.
- Talk about the different tasks
    point out high frequency words which can be built
    point out key words and phrases
    practise writing new letter.
- Work on related phonics and spelling.
- Vocabulary development.

2
- Vocabulary - revise star words
    introduce new one
    play games with flash cards.
- Play suggested word games.
- Revise words learnt so far.
- Introduce new letter
    learn to write new letter
    build words with new letter.
- Introduce copymasters.

Hour, as follows. (You will find ideas for more detailed use in 'Ideas for working through the literacy hour with this book' opposite.)

1. Whole class shared text work (15 minutes)
In the first fifteen-minute segment, work with the children grouped round you. This is the segment of the lesson for using a common text to develop a whole range of skills, including the teaching of word level skills, in context. When you intend to concentrate on a particular letter string as the focus for a lesson, write the letter string to be learnt on the blackboard or large sheet of paper. Work on the text of a book that freely uses words with the letter string being learnt. Read the story to the children then read it together, discussing the text, identifying and counting the number of words containing the new letter string, exploring word order and sentence structure.

2. Whole class focused word work (15 minutes)
During this segment of the lesson write the letter string several times, explore word building and word patterns, play word games with it, match the letter string sound visually and orally. Build words using the flash card letters and form sentences also using the Star words learnt to date.

3. Group and independent work (20 minutes)
This is the segment of the lesson when the copymasters will actively be used. Children should work on the copymasters for the letter string and use resources in the general copymasters where appropriate. You can work with the groups who need your support while keeping an overview of those children working individually. The copymasters follow consistent patterns and tend to use repeated instructions so that most children soon learn what is expected of them and can begin to work independently.

4. Whole class review session (10 minutes)
In the final ten minute segment go through the work you have accomplished.

Ideas for working through the literacy hour with this book

Here are some ideas for working through the literacy hour in detail with *Platform Phonics*.

Whole class text level work
- Read a big book together several times, pointing to each word as you read it.
- Read it again asking children to tell you when you read a word that they know.
- The children should join in the second reading with you or as soon as they can.
- Can they see any words that are the same? Are there any repeated phrases?
- Would it mean the same if the words were written in a different order?
- Write the words in a different order and ask the children to put them in an order which makes sense. Remind them that what they read must make sense.
- Which words in the story can they build?
- Create sentences on the board with the children providing the words and giving the spelling.

Other activities
- Label things around the room and on the display table which contain the letter strings already learnt. Write the labels together, saying the words slowly as you write them. Ask children to repeat each word as you draw your finger underneath it. Add to your labels sight words they know or words they can build.
- Say jingles, poems and tongue twisters, sing songs and nursery rhymes. Talk about the words in them and their meaning. Which words include a specific sound or letter string e.g. 'sp'? Which words can they build?
- Make a montage of words cut from newspapers and magazines which they found in the story. Can they make sentences from found words?

2. Whole class focused word work
Learning star words (irregular high-frequency words)
- Use the flash cards provided on Copymasters 92-95 to revise the high frequency words learnt so far. Some will have been learnt as Star Words and others built from known sounds.
- Make up phrases and sentences with words learnt so far.
- Children should write familiar words and letters sounds from dictation.
- Sort Star Words according to their initial letters or blends, final letters or blends, medial vowels, digraphs etc.
- Introduce the Star Word to be learnt on the new copymaster.

When children are faced with a new word they can use the S.T.A.R. approach:
- **S**ound the letters in an attempt to work out what the word says.

- **T**ake a close look at the word and study the letter shapes.
- **A**re there any letter strings or words inside the unknown word which they recognise?
- **R**ead the rest of the text and make a reasonable guess, getting hints from both the content and any pictures on the page.

Children can practise the new word by:
- looking for the word in papers and magazines, cutting them out and pasting them on to a sheet of paper.
- sorting the word from a mixed bag of words.
- looking for it in their reading books. How many times can they find it on a page?
- learn it through the Look, Visualise, Write and Check technique.
- making up sentences of their own to include the new word to show that they understand its meaning and usage.

Letter strings

Introduce the new letter string to be learnt. Make sure the pure sound of the letter is used, that is without a 'schwa' on the end e.g. a soft 'sp' sound not a hard 'spur' nor 'spuh'.
- Write the letter string on a folded piece of card and stand it on the display table.
- One by one hold up items from the display table. Ask the children to say its name and tell you whether they can hear the new sound in the word.
- Ask children for other words they know with this letter string in them.
- Are there other things around the room with that letter string in them?
- Does anyone's name begin with that sound?
- Sort word cards according to the initial, medial or final letter or letter string.

Other word and letter activities

Play memory and word games (using only the short vowel sound):
- Say a word slowly made from letters they know. Repeat it two or three times. Ask the children to identify the letter sounds they hear and the word the letters make.
- Hold up an object or a card with a letter string on it and ask children for as many items as they can think of beginning with that sound or with that sound in them.
- Encourage children to use the letter sounds they know to help them decipher unknown words in their reading.

- Make word searches similar to the ones on the copymasters.
- Write large letters on card and share them out for children to hold. Have more than one copy of the letters. Ask them to come out if they have the letters which are part of a specific word. Ask them to stand in the correct order for their cards to spell the word.
- Listen for the sound in common in a group of words e.g. 'spot', 'spill', 'spread'. What is that sound? Children can offer words that begin with the same sound and go on to suggest a trio of words beginning with another sound.
- Ask children to write letter sounds and simple words from dictation. Use words that have been taught or ones which can be worked out from sounds already known.
- Show the letter cards slowly, one at a time for the children to write down. The first one to form a word gets a point. Keep the game short, about five minutes duration.
- Make up simple crosswords using picture clues.
- Ask children to make lists of all the words they know so giving them confirmation of what they know and confidence in their growing skill.
- Prepare children for any activity in the copymaster which may be new by working through samples on the blackboard.

3. Group and independent work

Introduce the day's copymaster. Talk about the letter string to be learned and how it is written. Go through the tasks to ensure that children understand what they have to do. Children should be able to work through the copymasters independently while you focus on the needs of one or two specific groups.

4. Whole class review

Gather the children round you and talk through what you have done together today.
- What have they done today?
- What new things have they learnt?
- Was there anything they are not sure of or did not understand?
- What did they like/not like about the work?
- Summarise and re-emphasise the day's teaching points.

USING THE UNITS AND GENERAL COPYMASTERS

The copymasters are organised into thirteen units of work. The copymasters build up from unit to unit to develop phonic learning and can be supported by use of the general copymasters from 92 on.

Because the instructions for using the copymasters are largely self-evident in *Platform Phonics 2* we have decided not to write detailed notes on each unit but to explain the general principle behind the copymasters here.

Structure of the copymasters

Each copymaster covers one sound and is structured into two or three discrete activities, as on the example on the right:

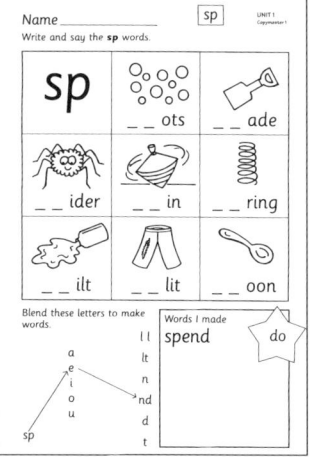

The top half usually introduces the sound and can be tackled in the following way, depending on how independently children are working on the page. (As children get experience of *Platform Phonics* you will find that they will be able to work largely independently during the Literacy Hour independent sessions.)

- Identify the sound to be learned by the children.
- Ask children to think of words beginning or ending with this sound.
- Go through the words and pictures with the children. Ask them to say the word then write the missing letters in the spaces.

The bottom half of the page usually contains two activities: a word search or blending task and a right hand side box for children to practise writing words. The writing box is an opportunity to write words they have made through blending activities on the page or to write words from other sources.

The star word is usually at the bottom right of the page. The star word can be learned in several ways. This can be done by cutting out and collecting the star words in photocopiable fold-up booklets on the last page of this book, reinforcing the star words through other classroom activities or using the photocopiable word sheets at the back.

(You have the option of suppressing this feature by blotting out the star word on a copy of the master before you make copies for the children. However, in practice, many teachers will want to take up the option of adding this extra dimension of learning as they go along.)

Sometimes the bottom half of a sheet is given to a word wall:

Children can either rewrite and read back words which they have written in the top half of the page in the word wall or you can differentiate the level of the activity by asking some children to go to other sources to find words with the relevant sound e.g. dictionaries, their reading books or print around the classroom.

Variety into the sound activities on the copymasters is also introduced through the use of word wheels. The lower circle should be cut out and fastened to the circle in the box with a split brass fastener. The inner wheel can then be turned to make words. (If you wish you can have one spare sheet to be cut up in this way for group work, whilst individual children keep their own sheets intact; or children can rotate the smaller circle within the larger one without permanently fixing it.)

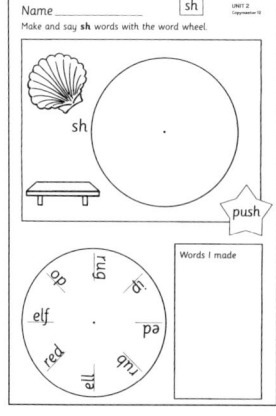

Learning maps

At the end of each unit you will find a learning map. This provides an assessment opportunity and a chance to sum up the work of the unit. Usually there are about three or four activities on the learning map which will give you a good idea how much the children have absorbed.

The learning maps always start by asking children

to write star words from memory. They may not be able to remember what star words they have learned. They could carry out a look/cover/write/check routine here in conjunction with the fold-up word book at the back, or other sources. (You may for example have used the star words within the classroom environment in some way.) You may want to have a session going over the star words before they do this.

The activities after the star words provide a range of writing and blending activities to double check the learning of the unit. This usually involves at least one activity writing words with the relevant blends. Children can either write these words from memory or by researching words in the classroom, or they could go back to previously completed copymasters to hunt for relevant words. You can differentiate the difficulty of learning map tasks for different groups.

Contents of the units

Unit 1
Unit 1 introduces three common letter strings used both at the beginning and the end of words. Using these sounds with the short vowel and consonant sounds learnt in *Platform Phonics 1* another fifty words are added to children's vocabulary.
Sounds covered: sp -sp st -st sk -sk
Star words: do last our.

Unit 2
The second unit introduces three common digraphs (plus two variations) used at both the beginning and the end of words. Using these sounds with the short vowel and consonant sounds learnt in *Platform Phonics 1* another hundred words are added to children's vocabulary.
Sounds covered: th thr -th ch -tch sh -sh
Star words: their once push old white.

Unit 3
This third unit introduces five more consonant blends made by adding other consonants to 's'. Children have already covered blends 'sp' and 'st' in the first unit.
Sounds covered: sc scr sm sn squ sw
Star words: don't can't because.

Unit 4
This fourth unit introduces six more blends made by adding 'l' to another letter.
Sounds covered: bl cl fl gl pl sl
Star words: these many want

Copymaster 26: the five words in 'planet' are 'plan', 'plane', 'lane', 'an' and 'net'.

Unit 5
This unit introduces six more blends by adding 'r' to another consonant.
Sounds covered: br cr dr fr gr pr str tr
Star words: brother could should would
Copymaster 32: the three words in 'fragment' are 'rag', 'me' and 'men'.

Unit 6
Unit 6 introduces ten more blends, adding 'l' or 'n' to another letter. Sometimes two blends appear on the same sheet. This encourages children to listen carefully to the component consonant.
Sounds covered: -ld -lf -lk -lp -lt -ct -xt -xty -ft -pt -nt
Star words: sister other another four your.

Unit 7
Unit 7 introduces nine more blends and two digraphs: '-ng' and '-nk'.
Sounds covered: -mp -nd -ng -nk et en in on al el il ol
Star words: little night were people

Unit 8
Unit 8 introduces nine double letter sounds, adding 'l' or 'n' to another consonant. Two or three blends are on the same copymaster. This encourages children to listen carefully to the consonant sound.
Sounds covered: -dd -ff -gg -ll -mm -nn -tt -ss -zz
Star words: pull love

Unit 9
The five short vowel sounds were introduced in *Platform Phonics 1*. The remaining five units in *Platform Phonics 2* focus on the more complex vowel sounds and those affected by 'r'. This ninth unit introduces the long vowel sounds of 'a', 'i', 'o' and 'u' caused by marker or 'magic' e. Words with 'e-e' are not taught here because there are very few words in children's vocabulary which use this long vowel form except the words 'here' and 'there' which have been taught as Star words in *Platform Phonics 1*.
Sounds covered: a-e i-e o-e u-e
Star words;   live lived over

Unit 10
This unit introduces six double vowels of which the first four are diphthongs, plus the '-all' sound.
Sounds covered: ai ay oi oy ee ea all
Star words: eight half when called.

Unit 11
Unit 11 introduces four double vowel sounds and three diphthongs of vowels + w. Two pages are used for the different sounds of 'oo', only one is used for 'ow' but the Star word 'own' (Copymaster 74) opens the way for words like 'mow', 'row', 'sow', 'bow' and 'show' to be introduced.
Sounds covered: oo oo oa ou aw ew ow
Star words: blue who house own laugh

Unit 12
Unit 12 introduces vowels with 'r'. The letter strings 'are' and 'air', 'ear' and 'eer' are homophones in that they sound the same (as in 'fare/fair', 'dear/deer') but are spelt differently and have different meanings.
Sounds covered: ar are air er ear eer
Star words: where what water

Unit 13
This final unit introduces vowels with 'r'. Of the six, only 'or and 'ore' are homophones.

Using the general copymasters

Copymasters 92-95: High frequency words for flash cards and sentence building
All the sight words (star words) introduced in *Platform Phonics 2* are included here as well as all the other high frequency words that Year 1 and 2 children have to know. Copy the words directly onto card or stick onto card and cover them. Enlarge and use for classwork. Use for both flash cards and sentence construction.

Copymasters 96-97: Alphabet cards
These cards can be used for flash cards and word building. The letters are printed at the left edge to enable you to make a sliding motion as you join letters to make words and letter strings.

High frequency words check list
This is a check list for the words for Years 1 and 2 on List One of the National Literacy Strategy (page 61).

Star words fold-up book
This miniature booklet offers a highly enjoyable way of learning sight words. Children can cut out and stick in the star words from their copymasters to take home and learn. When learned they can colour the stars. If you do not want the copymasters cut up you can insert words yourself from the pages. Each fold-up book has space for fourteen words. To make the booklets:

- Photocopy a sheet for each child. Cut off the spare paper round the edge.
- Fold the booklet longways and cut along the solid line marked with the scissors.
- Unfold the sheet again; make an outward crease along the dotted line that runs from pages 2 to 3, and 6 to 7. Fold the book longways and bring the cover page and page 1 to meet pages 4 and 5 like this:

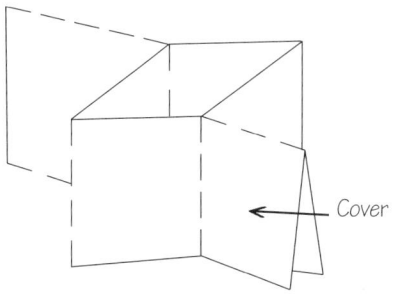

- Fold the back and front covers round to finish the book and hold together with a staple.

Name _____ sp UNIT 1 Copymaster 1

Write and say the **sp** words.

sp	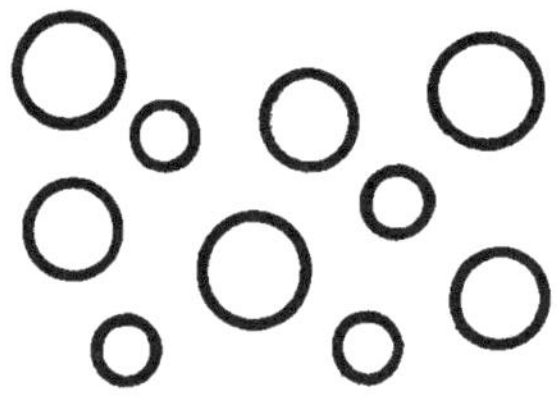 s_p_ ots	 s_p_ ade
 s_p_ ider	 s_p_ in	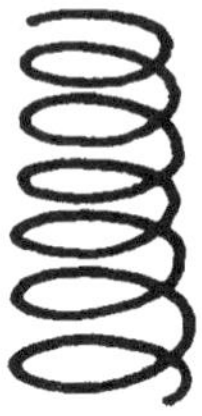 s_p_ ring
 s_p_ ilt	 s_p_ lit	 s_p_ oon

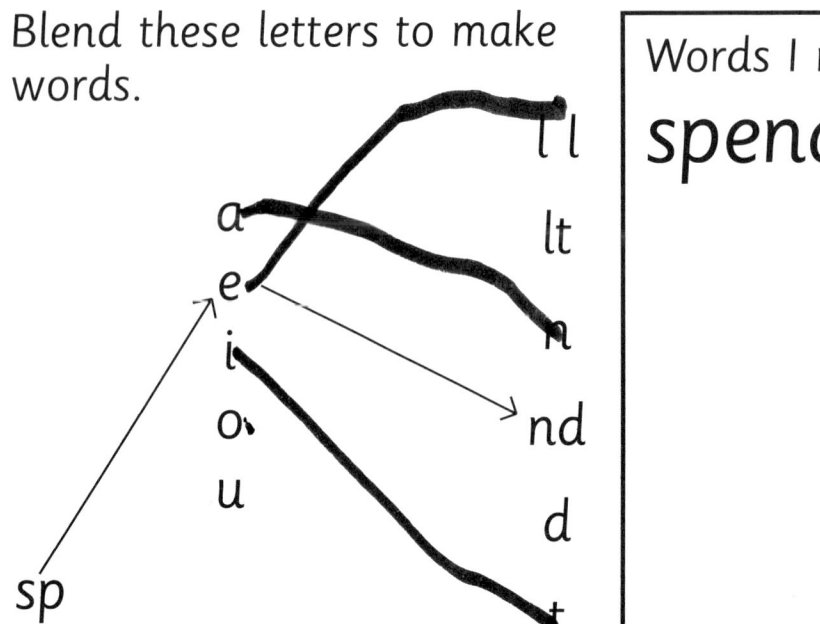

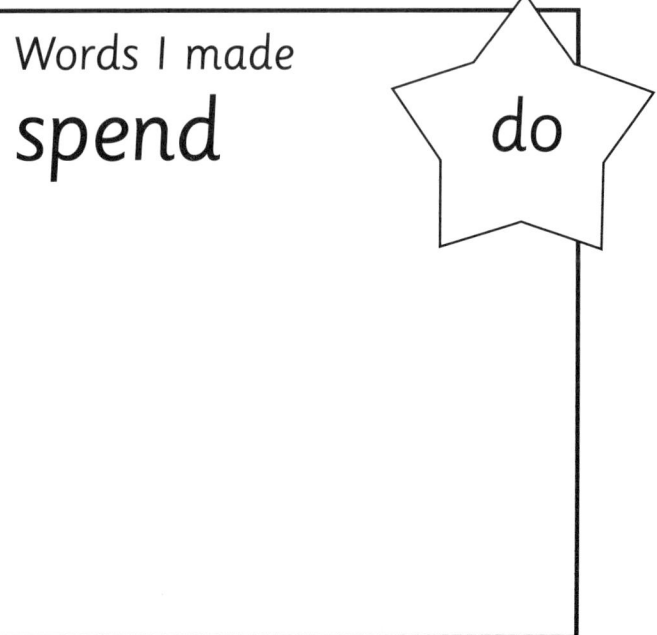

Blend these letters to make words.

sp → a e i o u → ll lt n nd d t

Words I made

spend

do

Name _____   -sp   UNIT 1
Copymaster 2

Write and say the **-sp** words.

ga **s p**

gra **s p**

cri **s p** s

wa **s p**

-sp

wi **s p**

cla **s p**

Word search

w	a	s	p	t	o
i	u	p	i	n	g
s	p	i	n	i	r
p	e	t	s	s	a
c	r	i	s	p	s
a	n	g	a	s	p
t	s	p	l	i	t

Words I found

wasp   do

Name _____

Write and say the **st** words.

st UNIT 1 Copymaster 3

_S_ _t_ ool

_S_ _t_ raw

_S_ _t_ _o_ _o_ _p_

_S_ _t_ air _s_

_S_ _t_ ump

_S_ _t_ _o_ _p_

last

Fill the wall with **st** words.

Name _____ -st UNIT 1 Copymaster 4

Write and say the **-st** words.

fir_st_

toa_st_

ch_e_s_t_

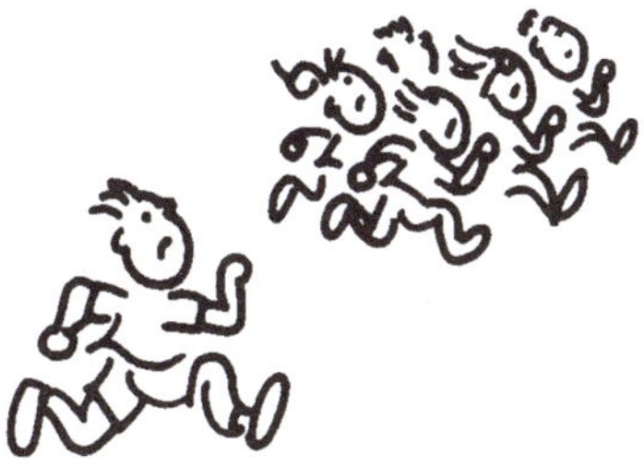

la_st_

-st

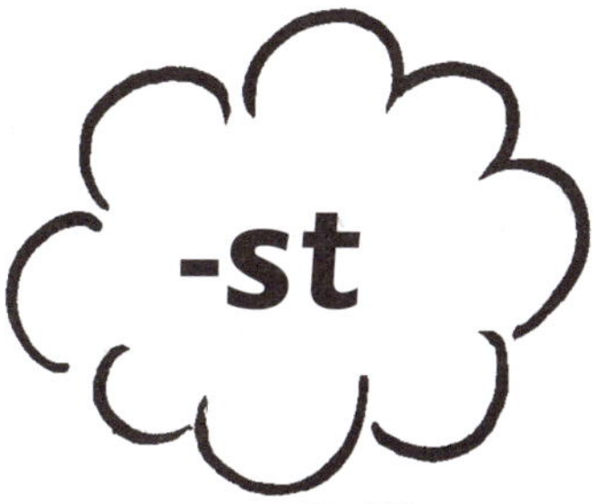

toa_s_t_er

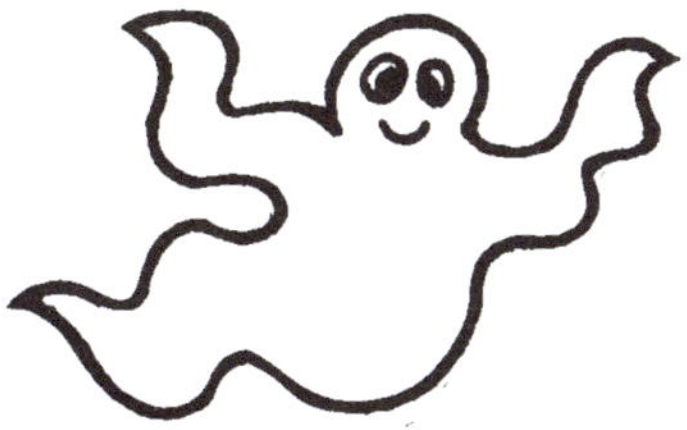

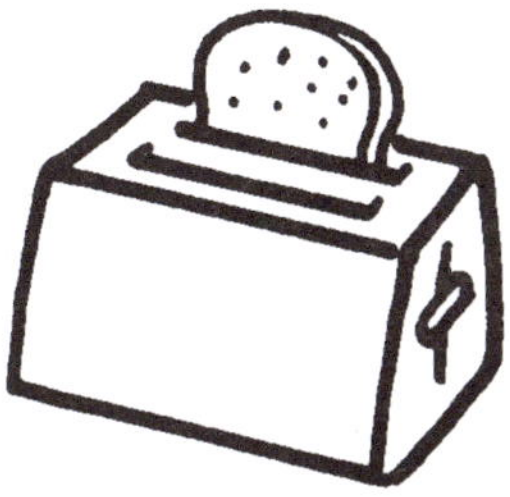

gho_s_t_

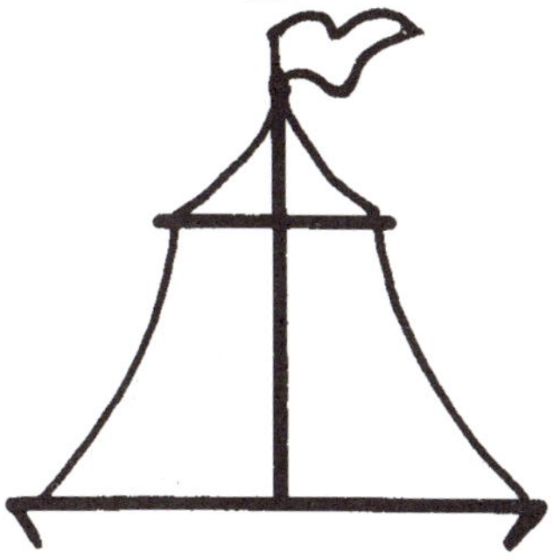

ma_s_t_

Blend these letters to make words.

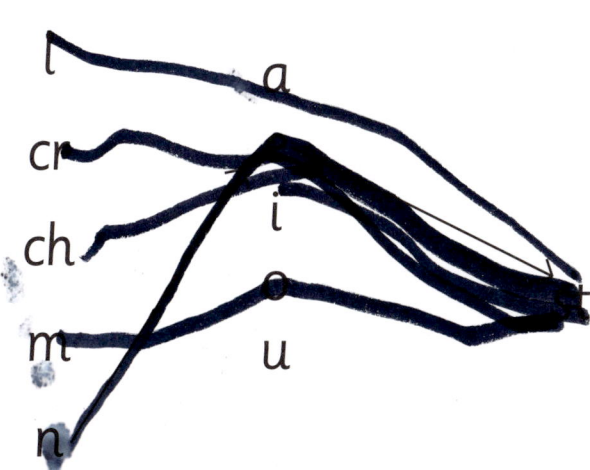

Words I made

nest

 last

Name _____

Write and say the **sk** words.

sk   UNIT 1
Copymaster 5

s k irt

s k unk

s k id

s k ull

sk

s k ates

s _ y

Blend these letters to make words.

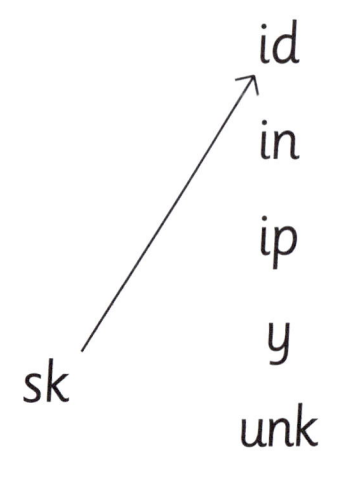

sk → id
   in
   ip
   y
   unk

Words I made
skid

our

Name _____   -sk   UNIT 1 Copymaster 6

Write and say the **-sk** words.

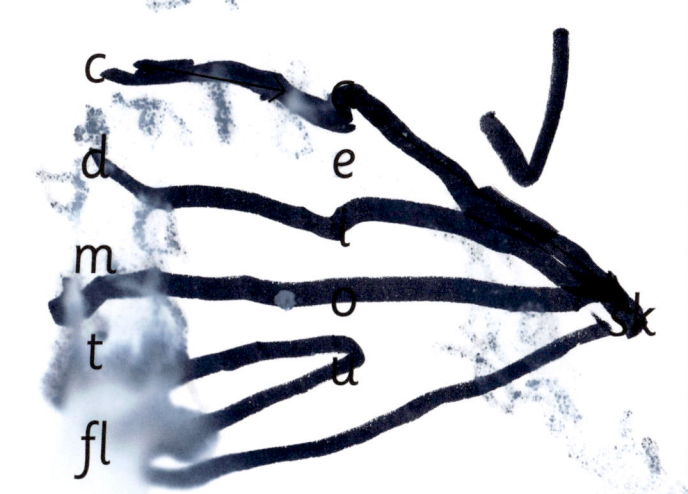

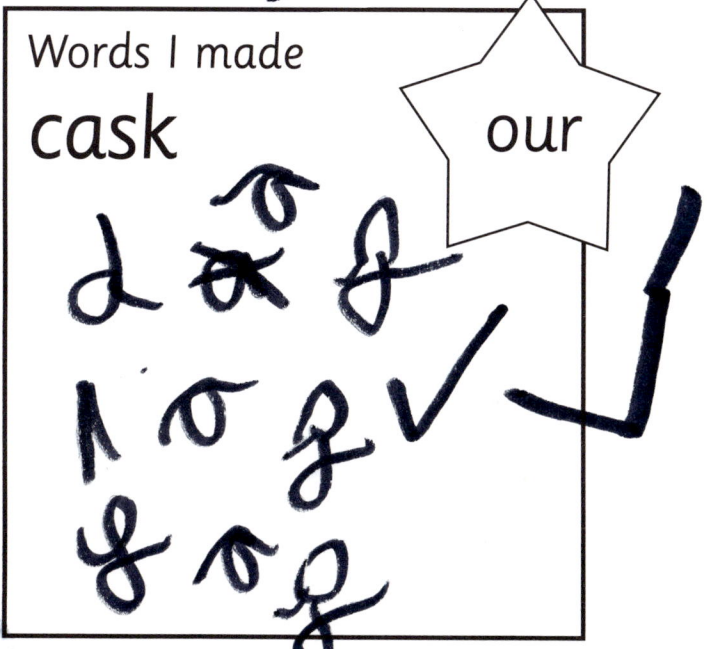

_e_ _l_ _e_ _s_ _k_ ✓   ma _s_ _k_ ✓   whi _s_ _k_ ✓

ba _s_ _k_ _i_ _t_   -sk ✓   _d_ _e_ _s_ _k_ ✓

wh _i_ _s_ _k_ er __ ✓

Blend these letters to make words.

c —
d — e
m — o
t — a
fl —

Words I made

cask

our

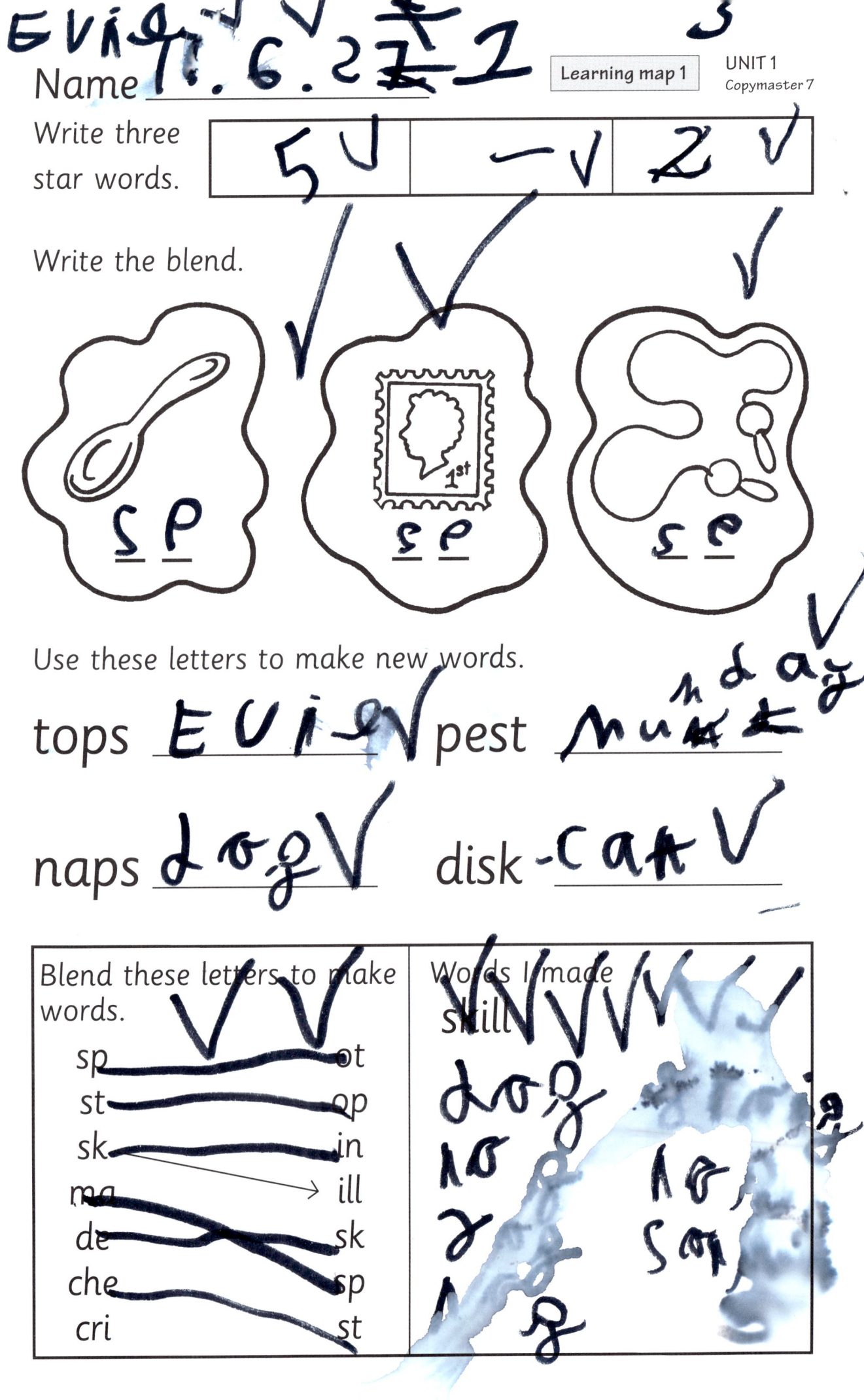

Name _____

th | thr

UNIT 2
Copymaster 8

Write and say the **th** and **thr** words.

t_himble t_h_r_ead t_h_r_ee

t_hirty **th thr** t_h_r_mb

t_h_r_ow t_h_r_tch

Say these words then add **t** at the front.

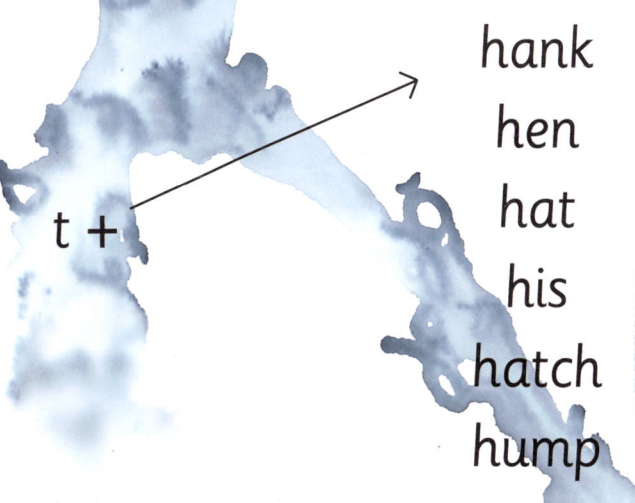

t + → hank
hen
hat
his
hatch
hump

Words I made
thank their

Name _____   -th   UNIT 2
Copymaster 9

Write and say the **-th** words.

ba _t_ _h_

t _e_ _n_ _t_ _h_

mo _t_ _h_

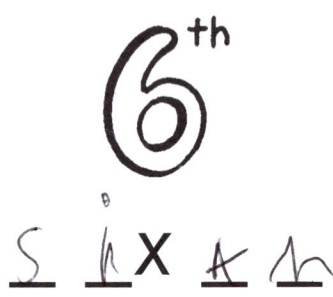
s _i_ x _t_ _h_

-th

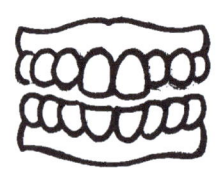
_t_ ee _t_ _h_

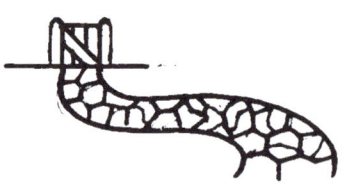
_p_ a _t_ _h_

Word search

m	o	n	t	h	s	s	p
a	n	n	o	d	t	i	a
t	o	o	t	h	e	x	t
h	i	t	n	i	n	t	h
s	e	v	e	n	t	h	s
a	s	o	u	t	h	e	o

Words I found

★ their

Name E vi? snh ch UNIT 2
Copymaster 10

Write and say the **ch** words.

ch	_ _ _ _ _	_ _ air
_ _ _ _ _	_ _ ain	_ _ eese
_ _ erry	_ _ _ n	_ _ ur _ _

Sort these **ch** words.

hicn	
niach	
pohc	
heeces	
etchs	
cipsh	

Words I know

once

Name _____   -tch   UNIT 2
Copymaster 11

Write and say the words ending in **-tch**.

 ha _ _ _	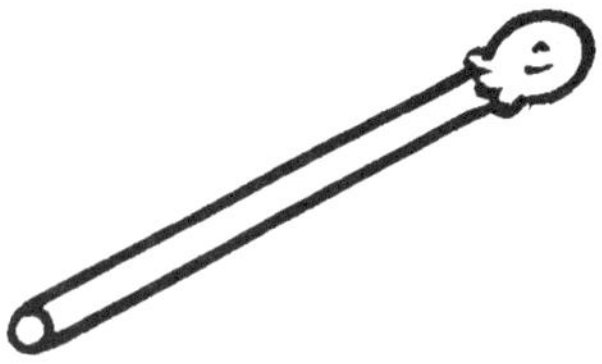 _ _ _ _ _	 h _ _ _ _
 _ a _ _ _	 _ a _ _ _	 p _ _ _ _
 th _ _ _ _	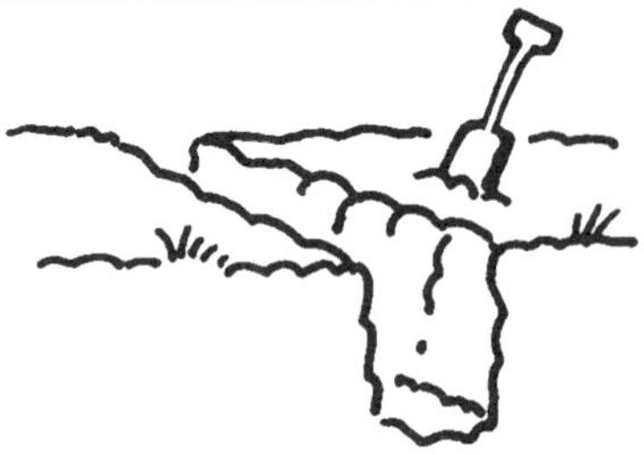 di _ _ _ _	 st _ _ _ _

Blend these letters to make words.

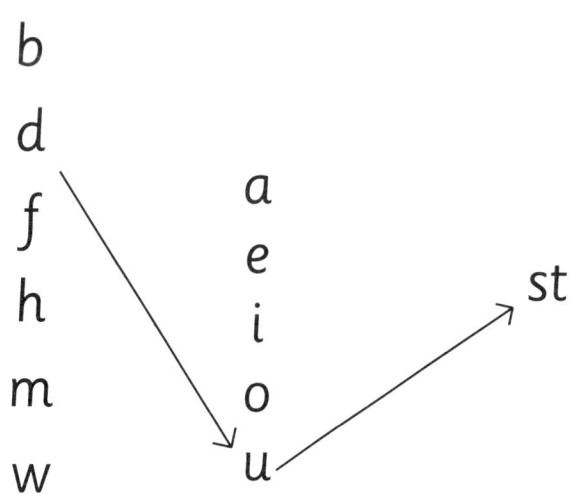

Words I made

dutch

once

Name _____

Make and say **sh** words with the word wheel.

sh

UNIT 2
Copymaster 12

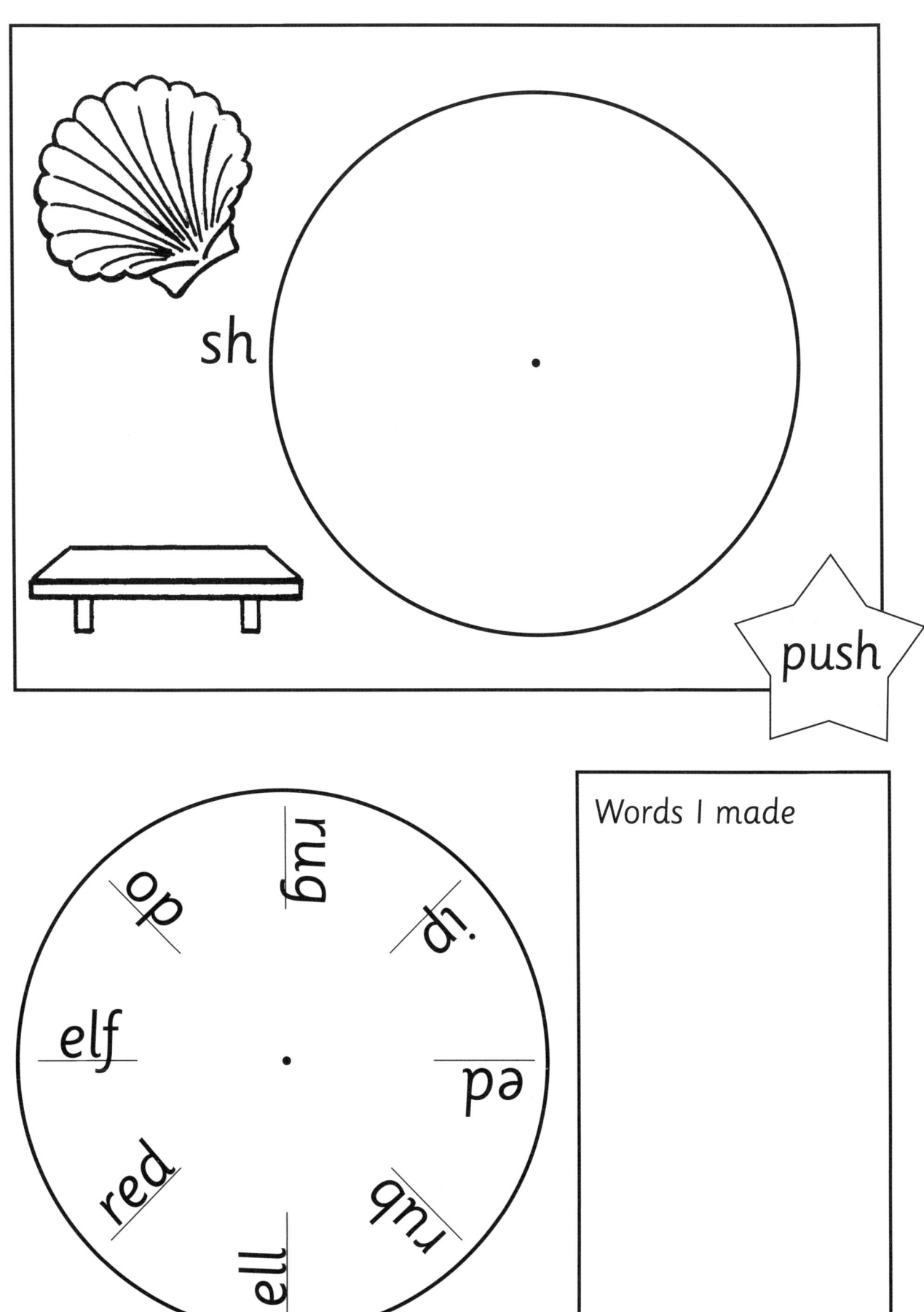

Name _____ -sh   UNIT 2
Copymaster 13

Write and say the **-sh** words.

spl _ _ _   wa _ _   squa _ _

Do the crossword.

Across   Down

2. 🥣   1. 🐟
3. 🌳   4. 🚢
5. ✂️   6. 🖌️

Blend these letters to make words.

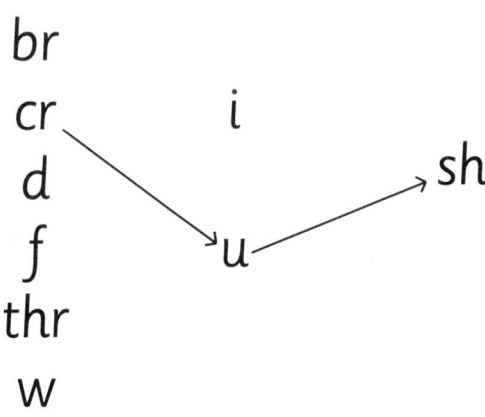

br
cr   i
d   sh
f   u
thr
w

Words I made

crush

old

Name _____   -ck   UNIT 2
Copymaster 14

Write and say the **-ck** words.

k _ _ _   r _ _ _ _

n _ _ _      _ _ _ _ _ en

p _ _ _ _ _

_ _ _ _ _ _

Blend these letters to make words.

ch   a   en
l   e
s   i → ck   et
st   o
p   u   y
t

Words I made

chicken

white

Name _____ Learning map 2 UNIT 2 Copymaster 15

Write three star words.

Fill in the blends.

_ _   _ _   _ _   _ _ _

Write five words for each blend.

th

ch

sh

-ck

Name _____ | sc | scr | UNIT 3
Copymaster 16

Write and say the **sc** and **scr** words.

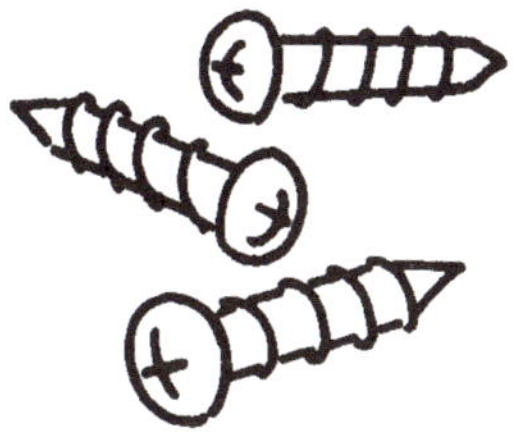

<u>sc r</u>ews   <u>sc</u> arf   <u>sc r</u>atch

sc
scr

<u>sc</u> ales   <u>sc r</u>ibble

<u>sc r</u>een

don't

Fill the wall with **sc** and **scr** words.

Name _____   sm   UNIT 3
Copymaster 17

Write and say the **sm** words.

_ _ ile

_ _ all

_ _ oke

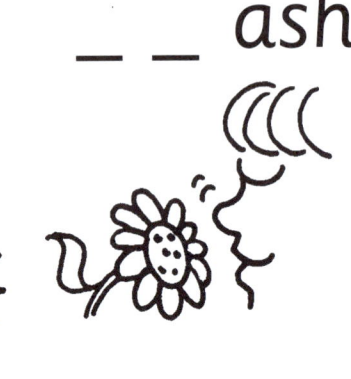
_ _ ash

sm

_ _ _ _ _

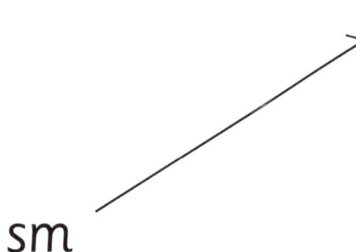
_ _ udge

Blend these letters to make words.

sm → ack
all
ash
ell
ith
ock

Words I made
smack

can't

Name _____

UNIT 3
Copymaster 18

Write and say the **sn** words.

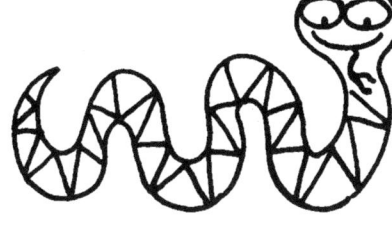
_ _ ake

_ _ ip

_ _ ai _

_ _ ow

_ _ ow _ _ _

Blend these letters to make words.

sn → a, o, u → b, ff, p, w, y

Words I made
snap

can't

Name _____

Write and say the **squ** words.

squ

UNIT 3
Copymaster 19

_ _ _ eeze

_ _ _ iggle

_ _ _ are

squ

_ _ _ irrel

_ _ _ id

Word search

s	q	u	i	r	r	e	l
s	q	u	i	g	g	l	e
q	s	s	q	u	a	r	e
u	q	f	s	h	o	p	e
i	u	i	s	q	u	i	d
n	i	s	q	u	a	w	n
t	b	h	s	q	u	a	d

Words I found

because

Name _____ UNIT 3 Copymaster 20

sw

Make and say **sw** words with the word wheel.

Name _____

Learning map 3 | UNIT 3 Copymaster 21

Write three star words.

Fill in the blends.

_ _   _ _   _ _   _ _ _

Add **s** to make new words.

_ nap   _ pot   _ can

_ lip   _ wept   _ till

Make lots of words with these letters.

```
        c
        k       a ──────→ d   lad
        l              ll
        m       e
        n              m
s       n       i
        p              n
        qu
        t       o      p
        w
                u      t
```

Name _____ bl   UNIT 4
Copymaster 22

Write and say the **bl** words.

_ _ indfold

_ _ ind

_ _ ade

_ _ ow

bl

_ _ azer

_ _ _ _

_ _ _ _

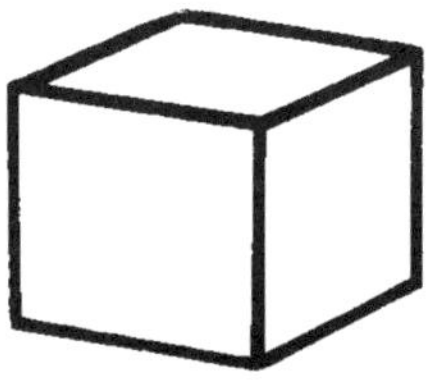

_ _ _ _ _

Word search						
b	l	a	c	k	b	b
l	b	l	o	t	l	l
e	l	e	t	i	e	a
n	u	n	o	n	e	n
d	e	d	a	n	d	k

Words I found

these

Name _____   cl   UNIT 4
Copymaster 23

Write and say the **cl** words.

_ _ _ _ _

_ _ ou _ _

_ _ ow _

_ _ oth

_ _ oa _

_ _ imb

Make **cl** words with these letters.

ilicnc	
mcplu	
lucb	
flicf	
coakl	
plac	

cl words

these

Name _____ fl   UNIT 4
Copymaster 24

Write and say the **fl** words.

fl	_ _ ame	_ _ ute
_ _ ower	_ _ y	_ _ _ _
_ _ oo _	_ _ _ _	_ _ ock

Make **fl** words.

fl	a / o	p	
fl	a / o	g	
fl	a / i	t	
fl	e / i	ck	
fl	a / e	sh	

Words I know

many

Name _____

[gl]   UNIT 4
Copymaster 25

Write and say the **gl** words.

gl	 _ _ ove	 _ _ obe
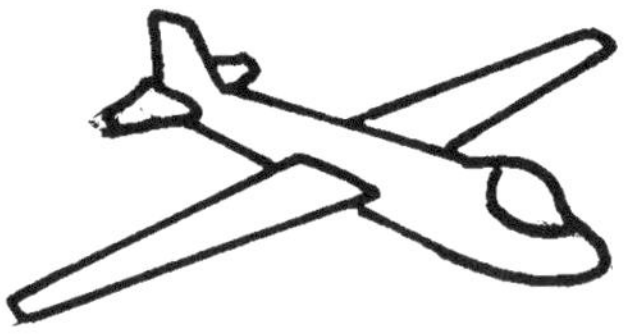 _ _ ider	 _ _ asses	 _ _ ue
 _ _ ass	 _ _ ad	 _ _ um

Blend these letters to make words.

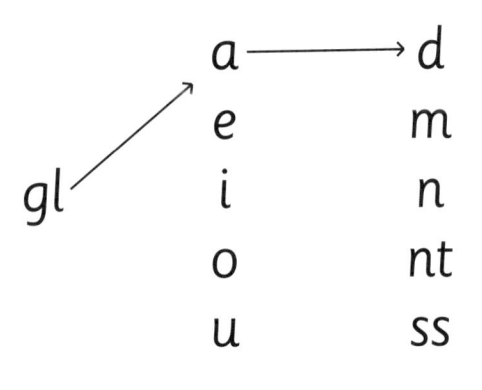

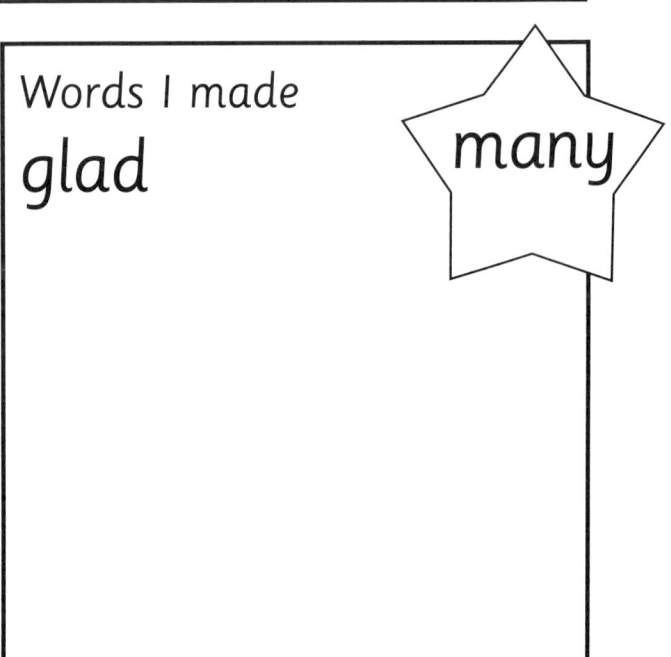

gl → a → d
     e   m
     i   n
     o   nt
     u   ss

Words I made
glad

★ many

Name _____ | pl | UNIT 4
Copymaster 26

Write and say the **pl** words.

__ __ ate   __ __ ane   __ __ ay

__ __ __ __   __ __ an __   __ __ u __

Find 5 words hidden in **planet**.

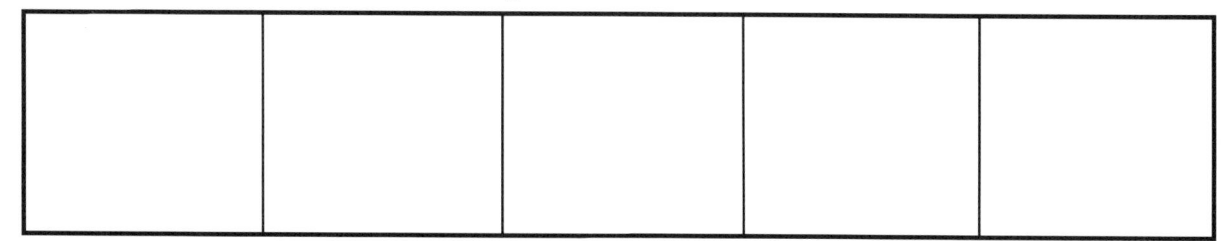

Word search

p	l	a	n	e	t	s	p
l	p	p	l	o	p	p	l
a	l	l	t	p	l	l	a
t	a	u	o	a	u	a	n
e	n	m	l	n	g	s	k
s	t	o	p	s	k	h	s

Words I found

want

Name _____ | sl | UNIT 4
Copymaster 27

Write and say the **sl** words.

sl	_ _ _ _ (slug)	_ _ ing (sling)
_ _ ide (slide)	_ _ _ _ _ (slugs)	_ _ edge (sledge)
_ _ it (slit)	_ _ _ _ (slip)	_ _ _ _ pper (slipper)

Make **sl** words.

basl	
sedl	
mlis	
psil	
tols	
tils	

sl words

want

Name _____

Learning map 4 UNIT 4
Copymaster 28

Write three star words.

Blend the sounds to make words.

Sounds: fl, cl, bl, pl, an, ot, ap, ock

Add **b**, **c**, **f** or **p** to make new words.

_ lap   _ lank

_ lug   _ low

_ late

Words I made

Name _____ | br | UNIT 5
Copymaster 29

Write and say the **br** words.

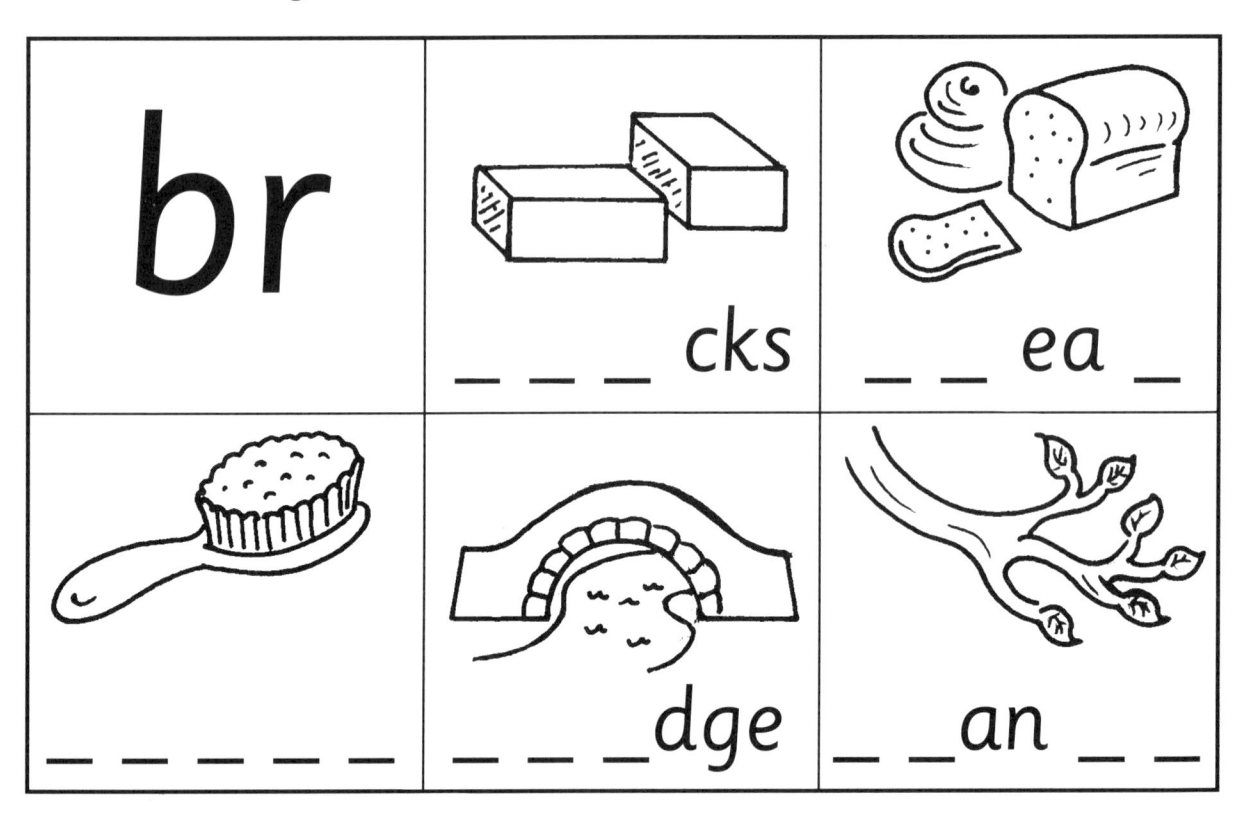

br	_ _ _ cks	_ _ ea _
_ _ _ _ _ _	_ _ _ dge	_ _ an _ _

Find four words hidden in **branch**.

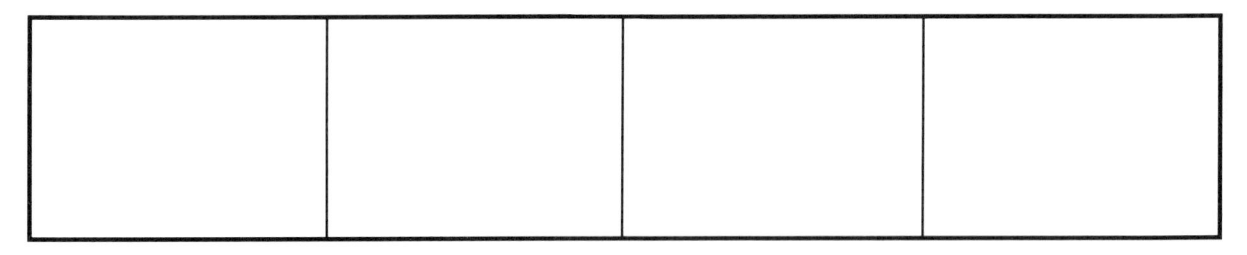

Say these words then add **b**.

b +
 ran
 rim
 rick
 ring
 rush
 ranch

Words I made

brother

Name _____ cr UNIT 5
Copymaster 30

Make and say **cr** words with the word wheel.

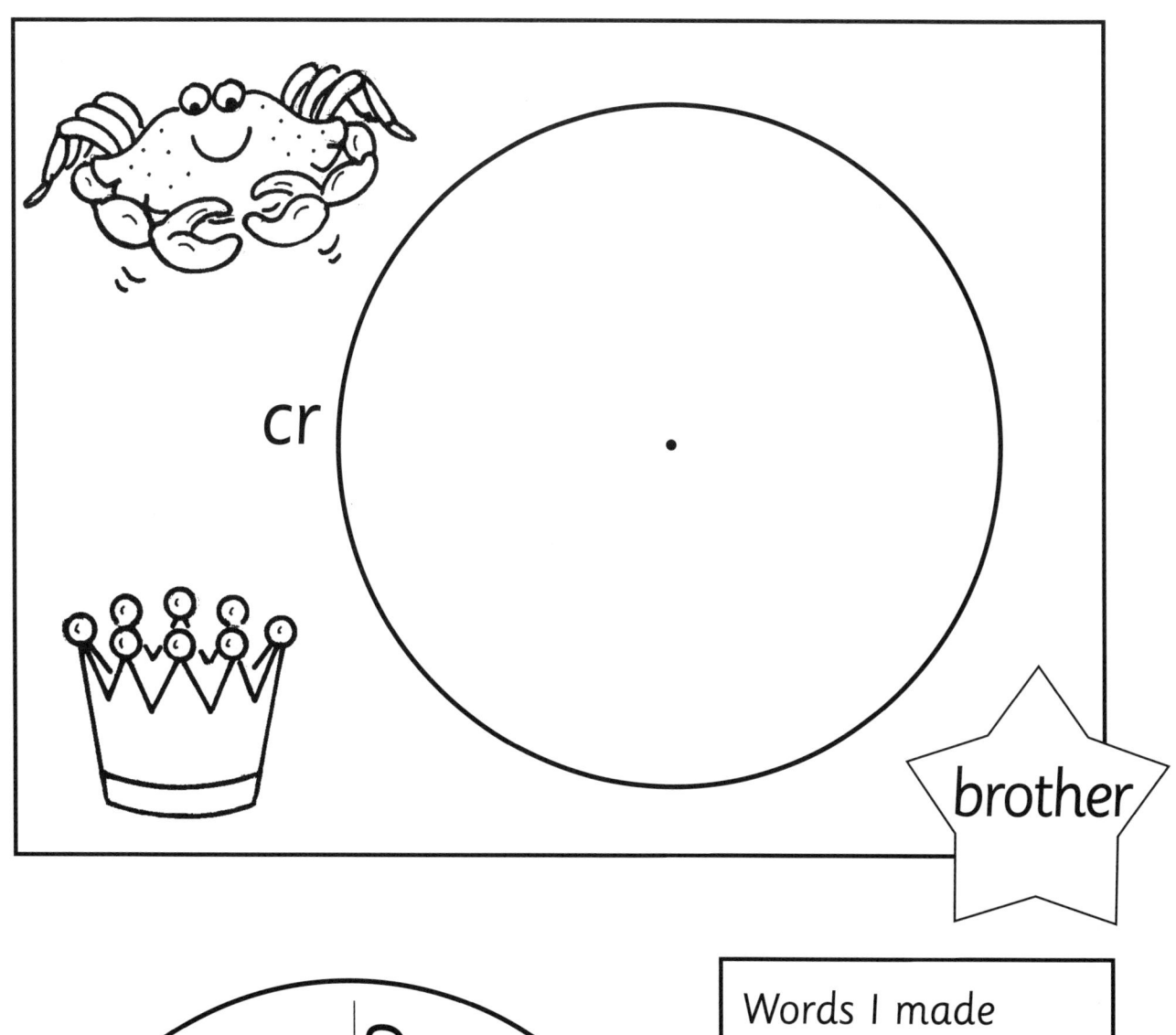

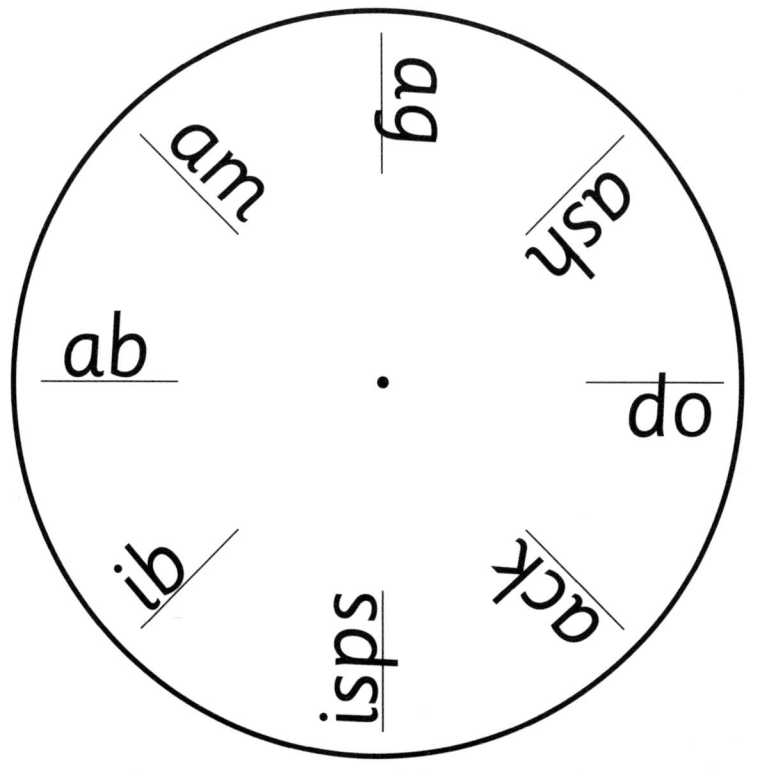

cr

brother

Words I made

am, ag, ash, do, ack, isps, ib, ab

Name _____ | dr | UNIT 5
Copymaster 31

Write and say the **dr** words.

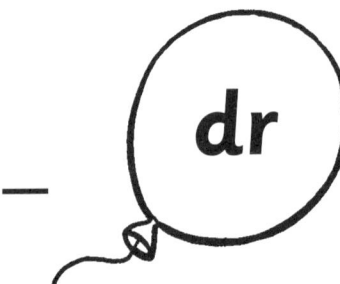

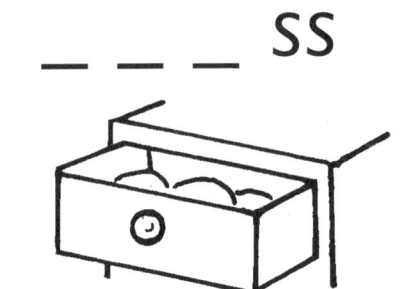

_ _ _ _   _ _ _ _ _   _ _ _ _ _

_ _ _ ss

_ _ _ _ _ _ _

dr

_ _ awer

_ _ _ _

_ _ ier

Say these words then add **d**.

d +   rag
      rain
      raw
      rink
      rip
      rum

Words I made

could

Name _____ | fr | UNIT 5
Copymaster 32

Write and say the **fr** words.

| fr | _ _ _ _ | _ _ idge |
| _ _ ui _ | _ _ ame | _ _ _ _ _ |

Find three words hidden in **fragment**.

Join the letters to make words.

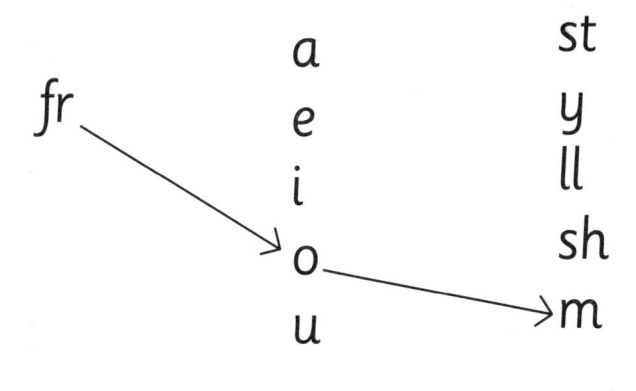

fr — a e i o u — st y ll sh m

Words I made
from

could

Name _____ gr   UNIT 5
Copymaster 33

Write and say the **gr** words.

_ _ _ _

_ _ ape _

_ _ ate

_ _ ab

gr

_ _ _ _

_ _ a _ _

Blend these letters to make words.

gr → a → ss
    e   b
    i   m
    o   nd
    u   n
         pe

Words I made

grass

should

Name _____   pr   UNIT 5
Copymaster 34

Write and say the **pr** words.

_ _ _ _

_ _ ism

_ _ int

_ _ _ sent

_ _ op

_ _ ize

Blend these letters to make words.

pr

a
e
i
o
u

m
nt
p
sent
sm
ss
ze

Words I made

prop

should

Name _____ | str | tr | UNIT 5
Copymaster 35

Write and say the **tr** and **str** words.

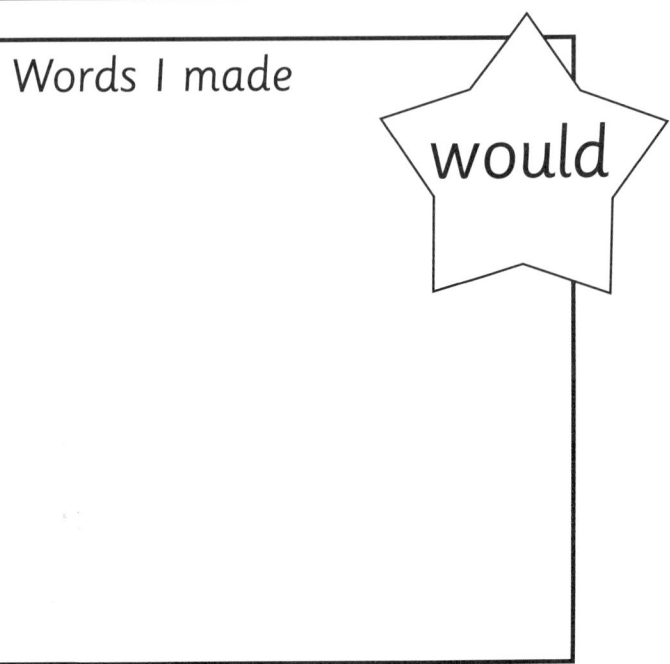

_ _ _ ee _	_ _ _ _ angle	_ _ _ ctor
_ _ _ ck	_ _ _ ipes	_ _ _ aw
_ _ _ _ _ _	_ _ _ ee _	_ _ _ ai _

Blend these letters to make words.

tr

    a   p
    e   t
    i   m
    o   ck
str u   nk

Words I made

would

Name _____   Learning map 5   UNIT 5
                                        Copymaster 36

Write three star words. [ ] [ ] [ ]

Fill in the blend.

_ _   _ _   _ _

_ _   _ _   _ _

Find the hidden words.

<u>brim</u>ful   **brim**   diagram   _____
scrabble   _____   afresh   _____
entrap   _____   humdrum   _____
reprint   _____   standard   _____

Write two words for each blend.

br _____ _____   fr _____ _____
cr _____ _____   pr _____ _____
dr _____ _____   tr _____ _____
gr _____ _____   str _____ _____

Name _____   -ld | -lf   UNIT 6
Copymaster 37

Write and say these words that end with **-ld** or **-lf**.

_ _ _ _ er    ch _ _ _   _ _ _

wo _ _

shie _ _

½

ha _ _

-ld
-lf

_ _ _ _ _

Blend these letters to make words.

b
g
h   a
m   e   ld
s   i
t   o   lf
w   u
sh

Words I made

bald

sister

Name _____ | -lk | -lp | UNIT 6
Copymaster 38

Write these words that end with **-lk** or **-lp** words.

_ _ _ _

_ a _ _

sca _ _

ta _ _

-lk
-lp

_ _ a _ _

_ _ a _ _

Blend these letters to make words.

m	a
b	e
p	i
s	o
h	u

lp

lk

Words I made

sister

Name _____

-lt

UNIT 6
Copymaster 39

Make and write these words that end in **lt**.

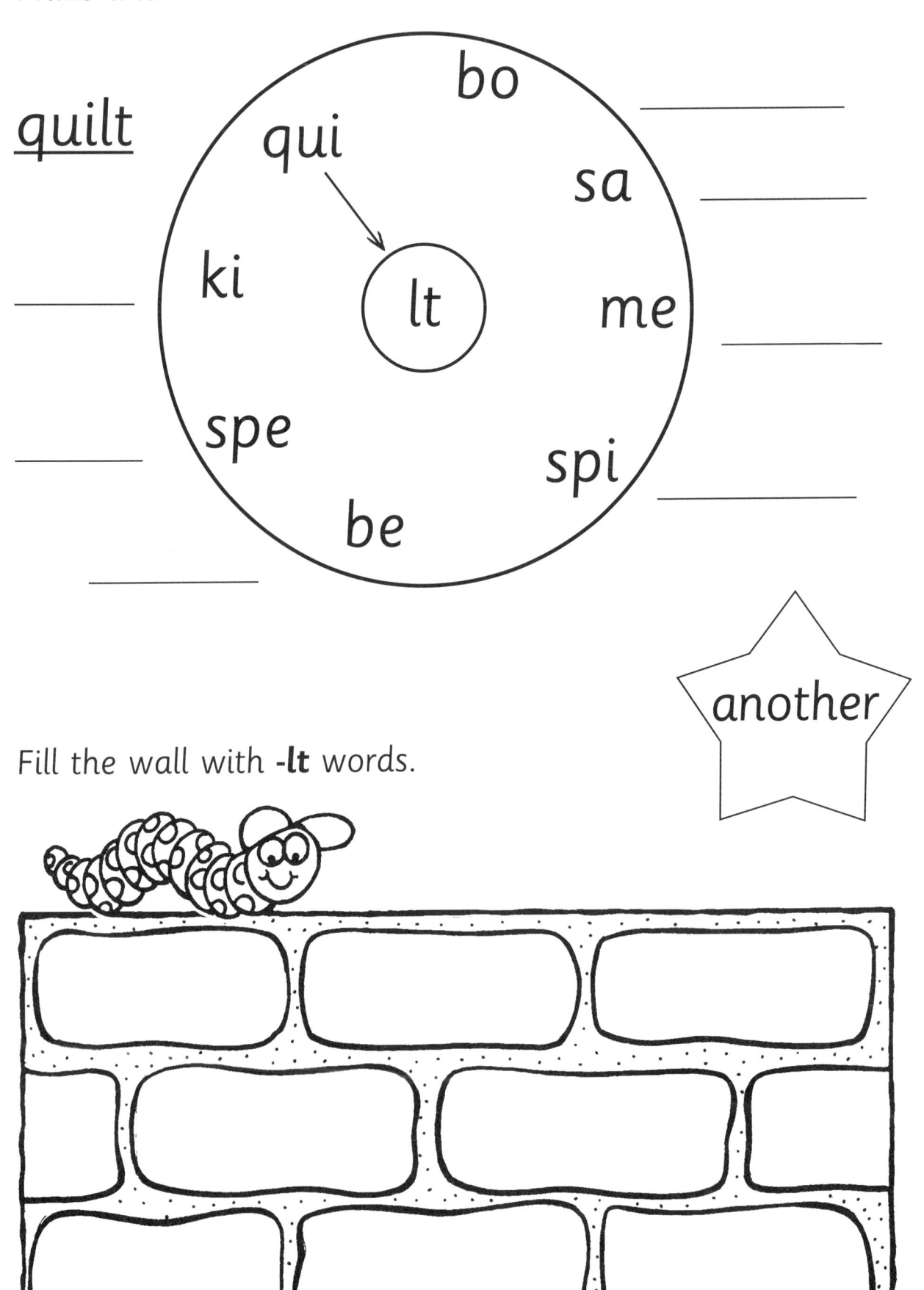

quilt

(word wheel with center "lt" and segments: qui, bo, sa, me, spi, be, spe, ki)

Fill the wall with **-lt** words.

another

Name _____ | -ct | -xt | -xty | UNIT 6
Copymaster 40

Make and say words with the word wheel.

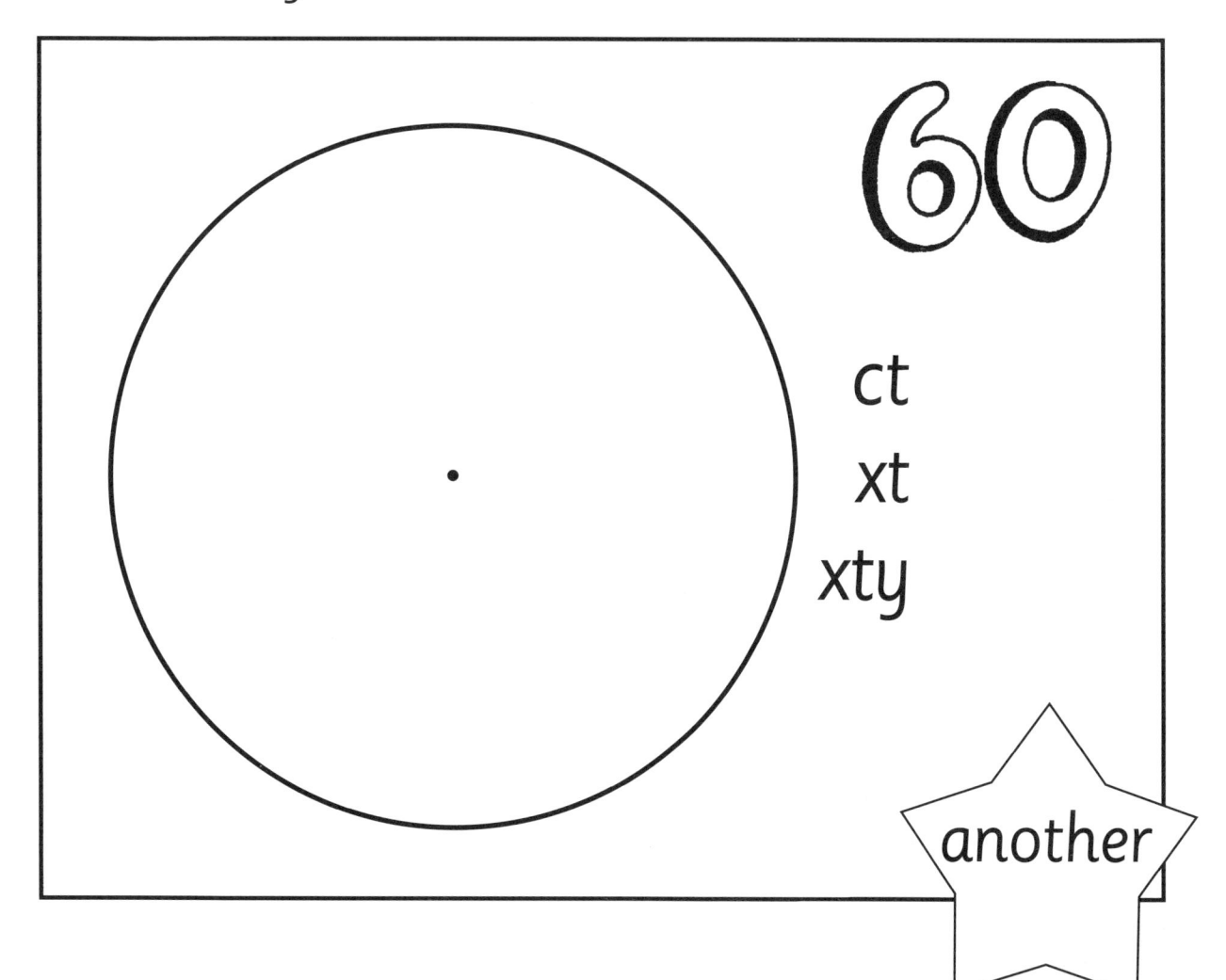

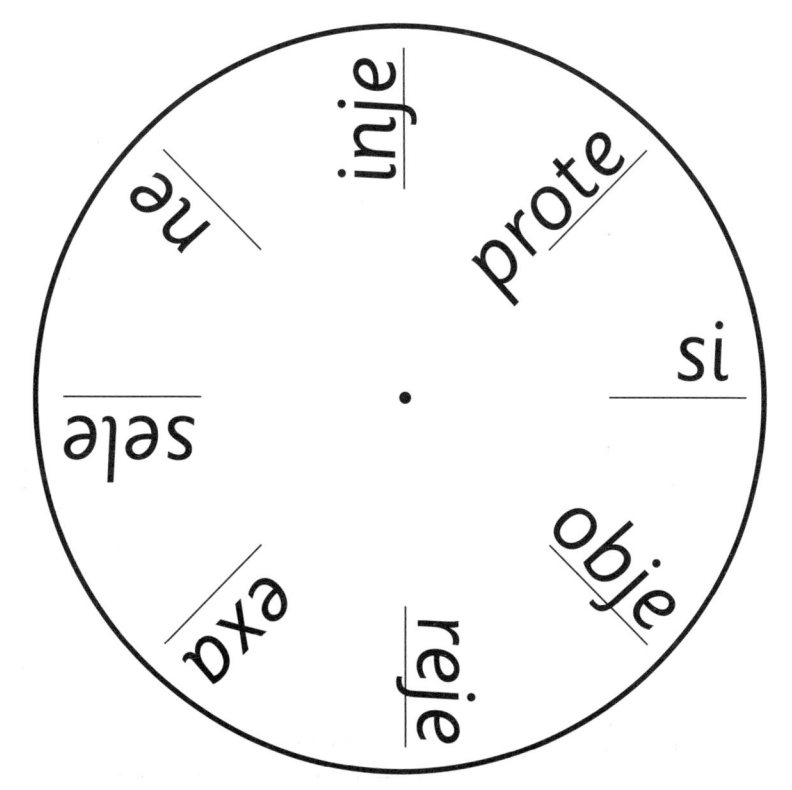

60

ct
xt
xty

another

Words I made

Wheel segments: inje, prote, si, obje, reje, exa, sele, ne

Name _____ | -ft | -pt | UNIT 6
Copymaster 41

Write and say these words that end with **-ft** and **-pt**.

g _ _ _

_ _ _ _ y

_ _ _ _

cre _ _

sle _ _

Blend these letters to make words.

l	a	
cr	e	ft
s	i	
sl	o	pt
	u	

Words I made

four
your

Name _____ |-nt| UNIT 6
Copymaster 42

Write and say these words that end in **-nt**.

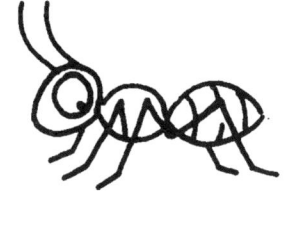

_ _ _

_ai_ _

_ _ _ _

-nt

gia_ _

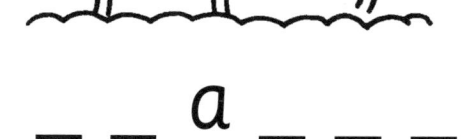

_ _ a _ _ _

Blend these letters to make words

b
h   a
m   e
p   i   nt
s   o
t   u

Words I made

four
your

Name _____ Learning map 6   UNIT 6
Copymaster 43

Write three star words. | | | |

Fill in the blends.

gia _ _

_ _ _

swe _ _

li _ _

Write three words for each sound.

-lf	-lk	-lt
-ft	-nt	-pt

Name _____ -mp   UNIT 7
Copymaster 44

Write and say these words that end in **-mp**.

mp	_ _ _ _ (pump)	st _ _ _ _ (stump)
cl _ _ _ _ (clamp)	i _ _ _ (imp)	_ _ _ _ (lamp)
r _ _ _ _ (ramp)	_ _ _ _ _ (stamp)	_ _ _ _ (jump)

Word search

l	u	m	p	s	j	i	g
i	f	a	c	t	u	m	s
m	e	n	l	a	m	p	s
p	d	c	a	m	p	m	m
t	r	a	m	p	e	a	u
b	u	m	p	e	r	d	m

Words I found

little

Name _____ |-nd| UNIT 7
Copymaster 45

Make and write these words that end in **-nd**.

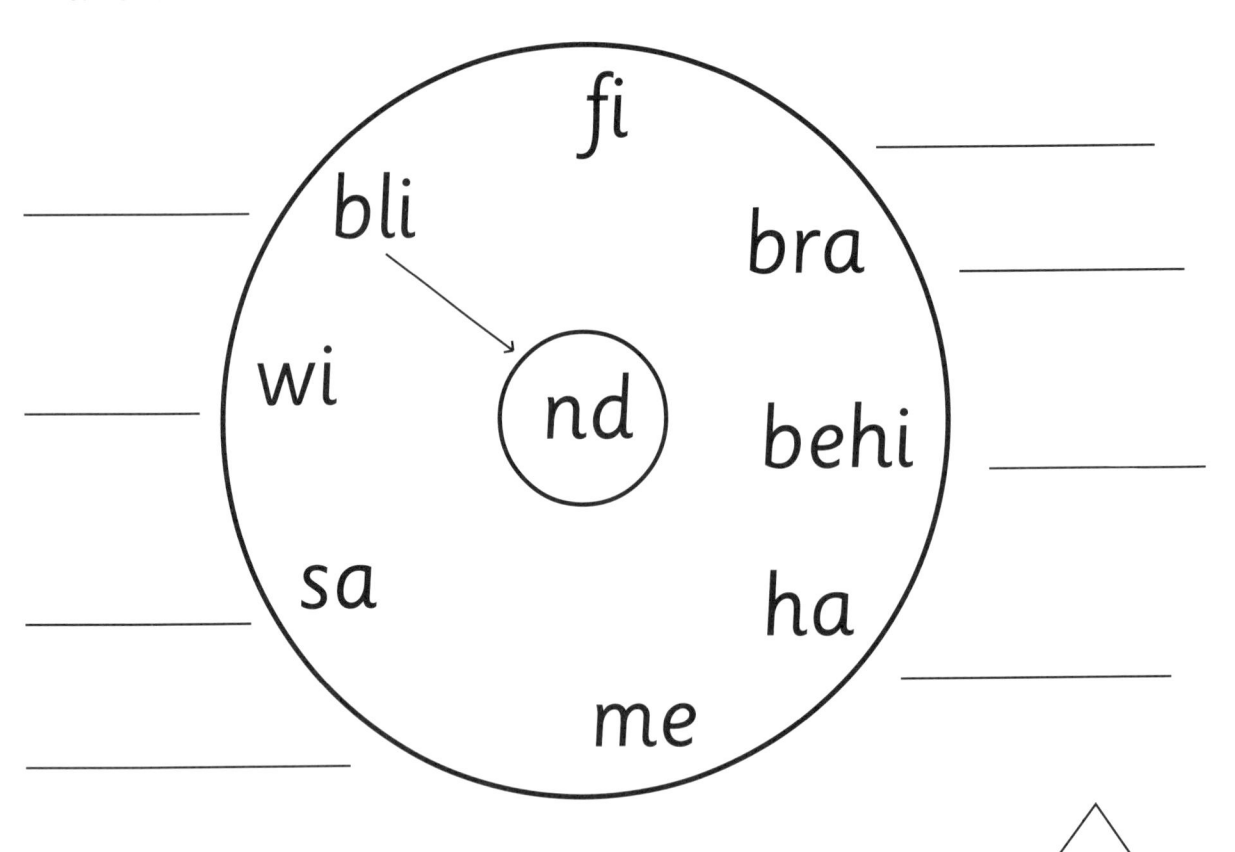

(word wheel with center **nd** and segments: fi, bra, behi, ha, me, sa, wi, bli)

Fill the wall with **-nd** words.

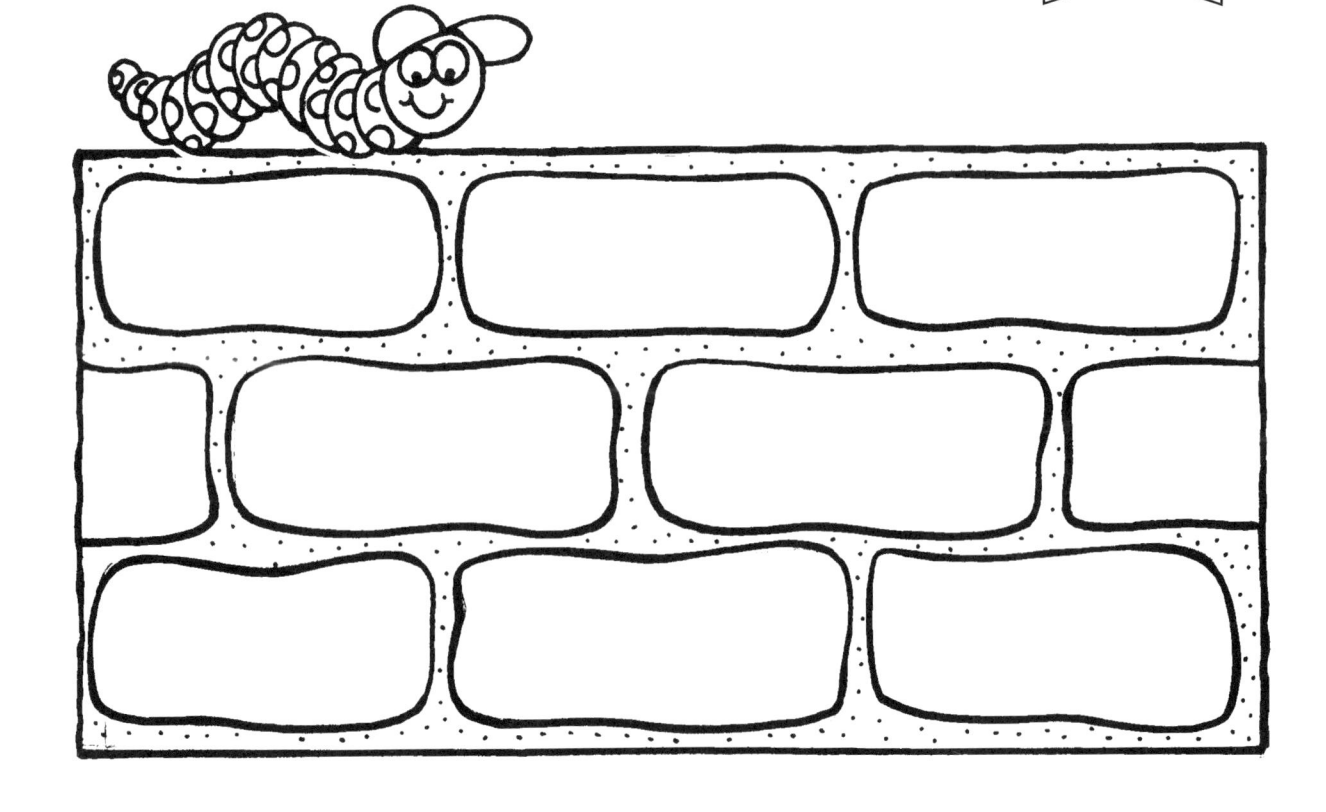

★ night

Name _____   -ng   UNIT 7
Copymaster 46

Write and say these **-ng** words.

_ _ _ _

_ _ _ _

_ _ _ _ _ er

ta _ _ le

_ _ _ _

_o_ _ ue

Make words with these letters.

act → ing

box   hav
end   play
giv   read
       go

Words I made

acting

night

Name _____

-nk UNIT 7 Copymaster 47

Make and say words with the word wheel.

nk

were

Words I made

Wheel segments: ba, ri, tha, si, su, dri, tru, ta

Name _____

UNIT 7
Copymaster 48

et

Write and say these **et** words.

_ _ ck _ _

_ _ _ _ et

_ _ _ h _ _

_ _ _ _ _ _

_ _ _ _ _ _

bl _ _ _ _

Blend these letters to make words.

b	a	ck	
cr	e		
h	i	lm	et
l	o		
p	u	nk	
t			
		bl	

Words I made

were

Name _____ | en | in | on | UNIT 7
Copymaster 49

Write and say these words that end in **en**, **in** or **on**.

_ _ tt _ _

_ _ tt _ _

l _ _ _ _

en

in   **on**

_ _ _ _ _ _

_ _ _ _ _ _

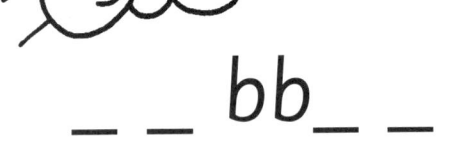

_ _ _ tt _ _

_ _ bb _ _

Word search

b	u	t	t	o	n	p	m
l	i	s	t	e	n	r	i
r	i	b	b	o	n	i	t
r	o	b	i	n	o	s	t
m	u	f	f	i	n	o	e
p	u	m	p	k	i	n	n

Words I found

people

Name _____ | al | el | il | ol | UNIT 7
Copymaster 50

Write and say these words. They end in **al**, **el**, **il** or **ol**.

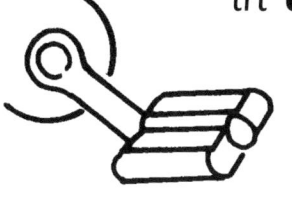

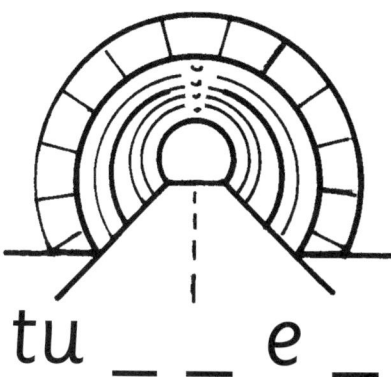

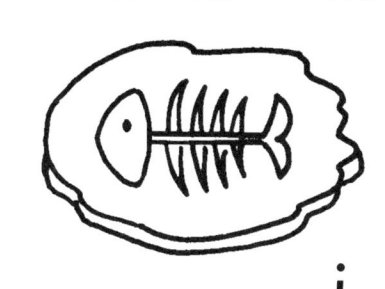

_ _ _ a _   (pedal)

tu _ _ e _   (tunnel)

_ _ _ e _   (camel)

_ _ _ _ i _   (fossil)

al
el
il
ol

_ _ _ _ a _   (petal)

_ _ _ _ o _   (petrol)

Blend these letters to make words.

f   a   d   al
p   e   t   el
c   i   m   il
t   o   nn   ol
     u   ss

Words I made

people

Name _____   Learning map 7   UNIT 7
Copymaster 51

Write three star words. [   ][   ][   ]

Find words for each blend.

-ng	-mp	-nk	-nd	et

Find the hidden words.

bangle _____   think _____
mended _____   dumper _____
flatten _____   cricket _____

Write two words for each blend.

-mp _____ _____   en _____ _____
-nd _____ _____   el _____ _____
-ng _____ _____   et _____ _____
-nk _____ _____   on _____ _____

Name _____ | -dd | -ff | UNIT 8
Copymaster 52

Write and say these **-dd** and **-ff** words.

2 + 3

a _ _

cl _ _ _ s

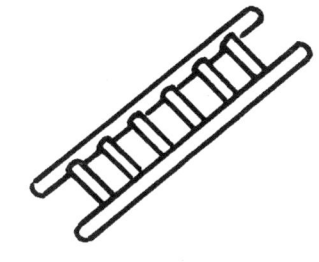

la _ _ er

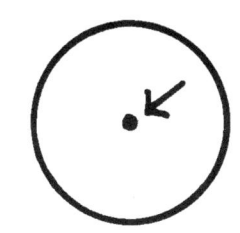

to _ _ ee

-dd
-ff

mi _ _ le

cu _ _ s

pu _ _ le

Blend these letters to make words.

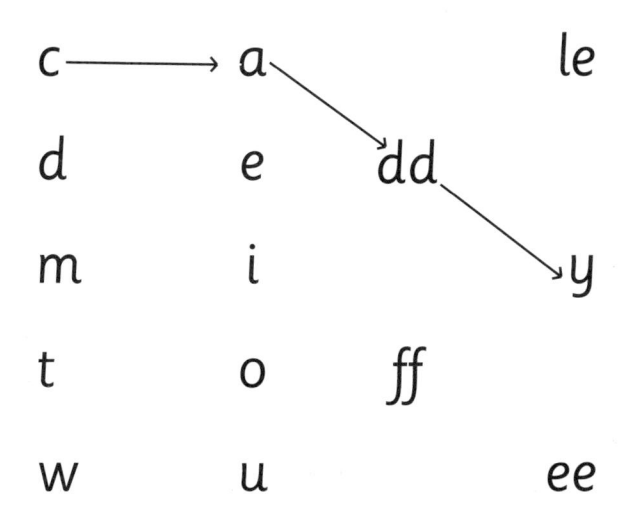

c → a   le
d   e   dd
m   i   y
t   o   ff
w   u   ee

Words I made
caddy
pull

Name _____ | -gg | -ll | UNIT 8
Copymaster 53

Write and say these **-gg** and **-ll** words.

e _ _	_ a _ _	_ _ _ _
_ _ _ _	-gg -ll	jo _ _ er
_ a _ _	_ _ _ _	di _ _ er

Blend these letters to make words.

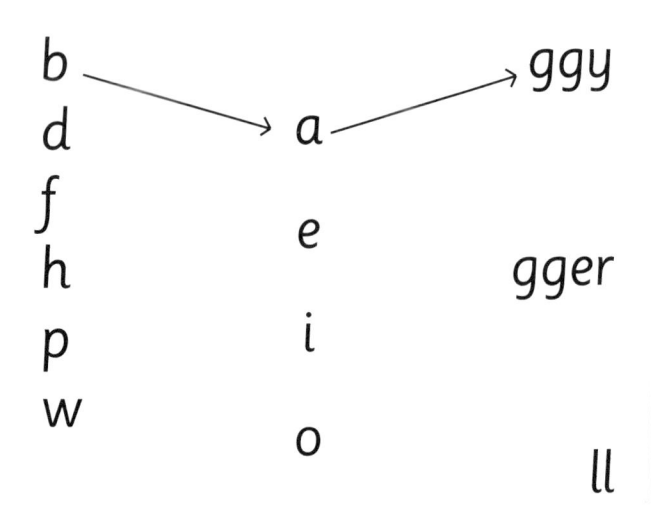

b
d   ggy
f   a
h   e
p   i   gger
w   o
          ll

Words I made

baggy   pull

Name _____ | -mm | -nn | -tt | UNIT 8
Copymaster 54

Write and say these words with **-mm, -nn** and **-tt** in them.

ca _ _ on

du _ _ y

ha _ _ er

bu _ _ on

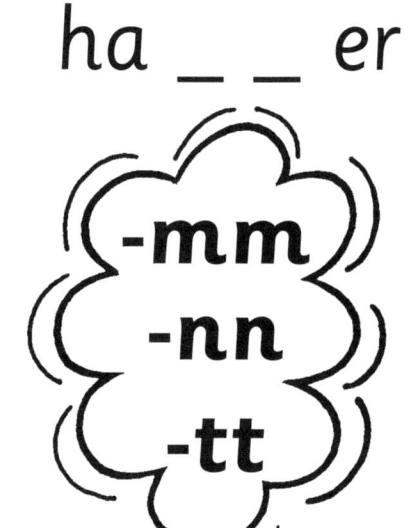

-mm
-nn
-tt

se _ _ ee

di _ _ er

ke _ _ le

Make words with these letters.

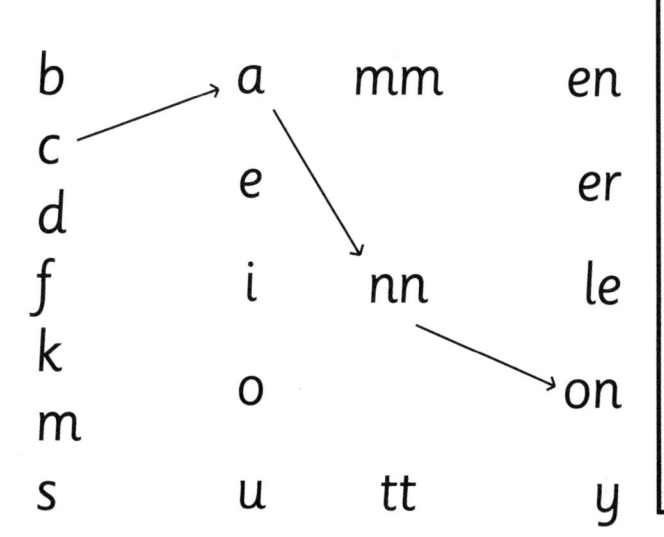

b   a   mm   en
c
d   e   er
f   i   nn   le
k
m   o   on
s   u   tt   y

Words I made
cannon

love

Name _____ | -ss | -zz | UNIT 8
Copymaster 55

Write and say these words with **-ss** and **-zz** in them.

fo _ _ il

_ _ _ _ le

_ _ _ _ y

-ss
-zz

_ _ _ _

_ _ _ _ le

love

Make **ss** and **zz** words.

siks	
esmsy	
azdlez	
sreps	
zuzb	
spsu	

More **ss** and **zz** words I found.

Name _____   Learning map 8   UNIT 8
                                                  Copymaster 56

Write three star words. | | | |

Fill in the missing letters.

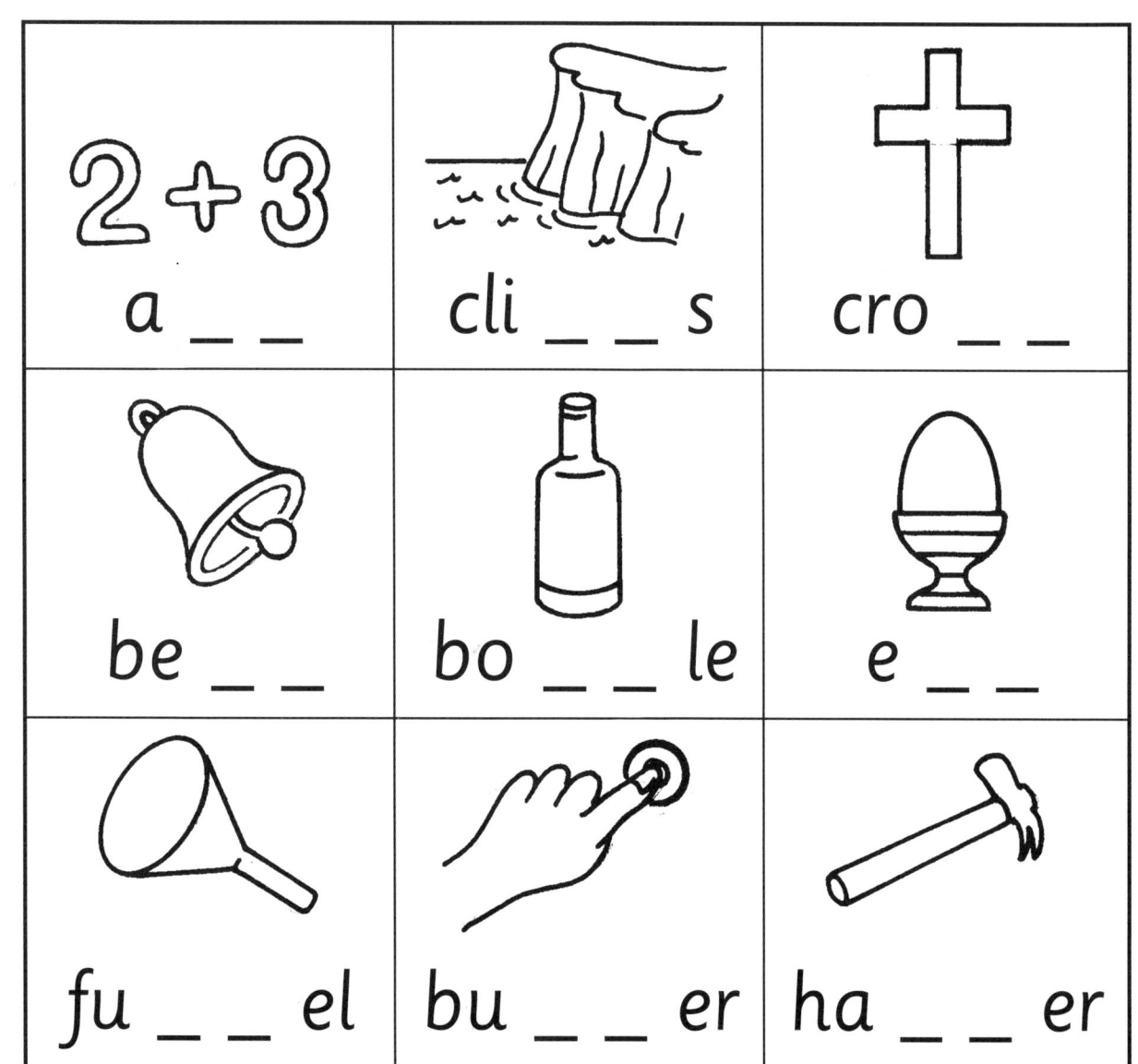

2+3 a _ _	cli _ _ s	cro _ _
be _ _	bo _ _ le	e _ _
fu _ _ el	bu _ _ er	ha _ _ er

Write one more word for each sound.

-dd		-ff		-gg	
-ll		-mm		-nn	
-ss		-tt		-zz	

Name _____

a-e

UNIT 9
Copymaster 57

Write the first word in each pair. Then write and say the **a-e** word.

_ a _ | _ _ _ _

_ a _ | _ _ _ _

a-e

_ a _ | _ _ _ _

_ a _ | _ _ _ _

live
lived

Fill the wall with **a-e** words.

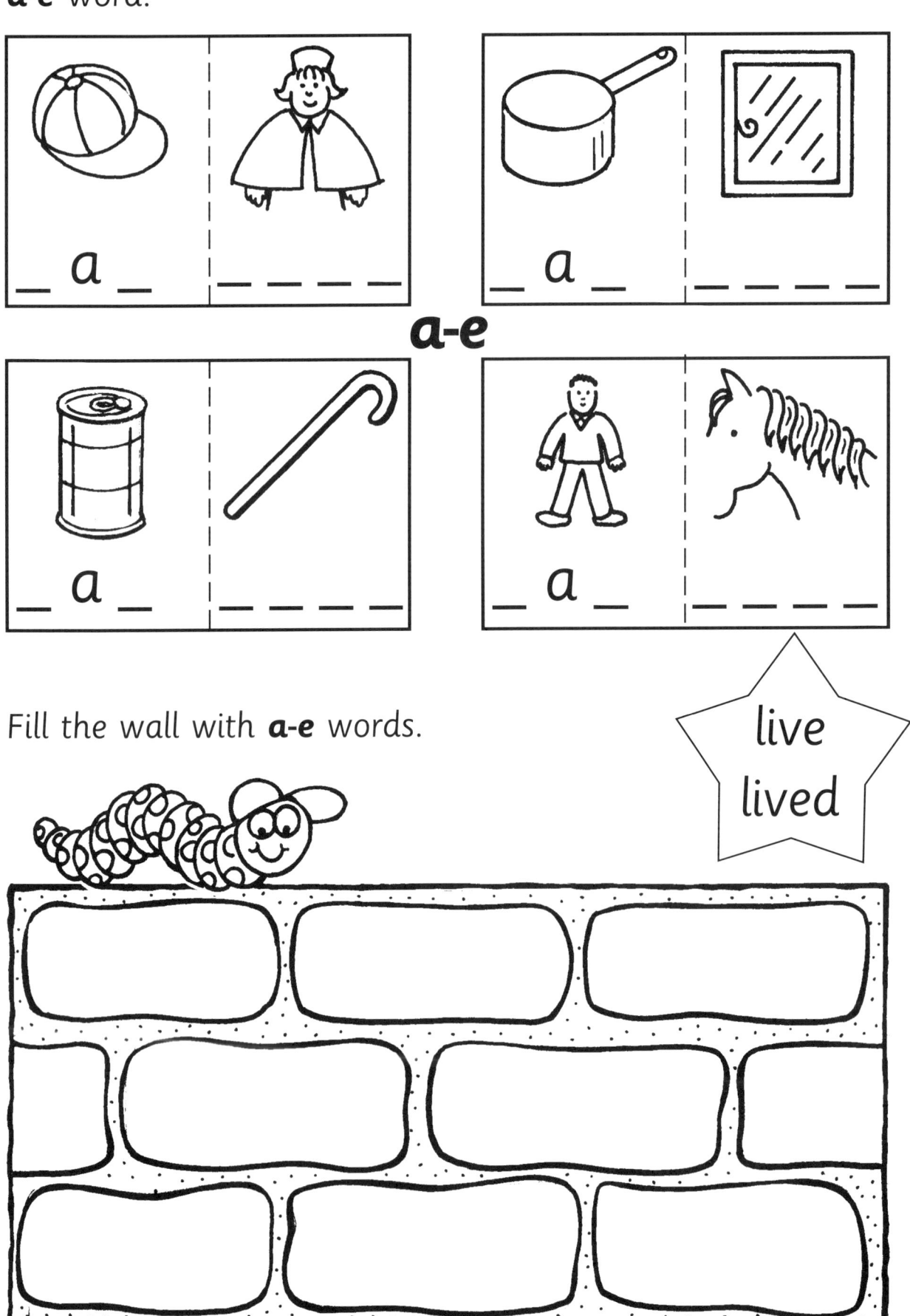

Name _____ | i-e | UNIT 9
Copymaster 58

Write the first word in each pair. Then write and say the **i-e** word.

_ i _   _ _ _ _

_ i _   _ _ _ _

i-e

_ i _   _ _ _ _

_ i _   _ _ _ _

Fill the wall with **i-e** words.

live
lived

Name _____   o-e   UNIT 9
Copymaster 59

Write and say these **o-e** words.

_ _ _ _

p _ _ _

_ _ _ _   o-e   n _ _ _

h _ _ _   _ _ _ _

Blend these letters to make words.

c
h   k
r   l
br   o   e
ch   p
sm   s
st

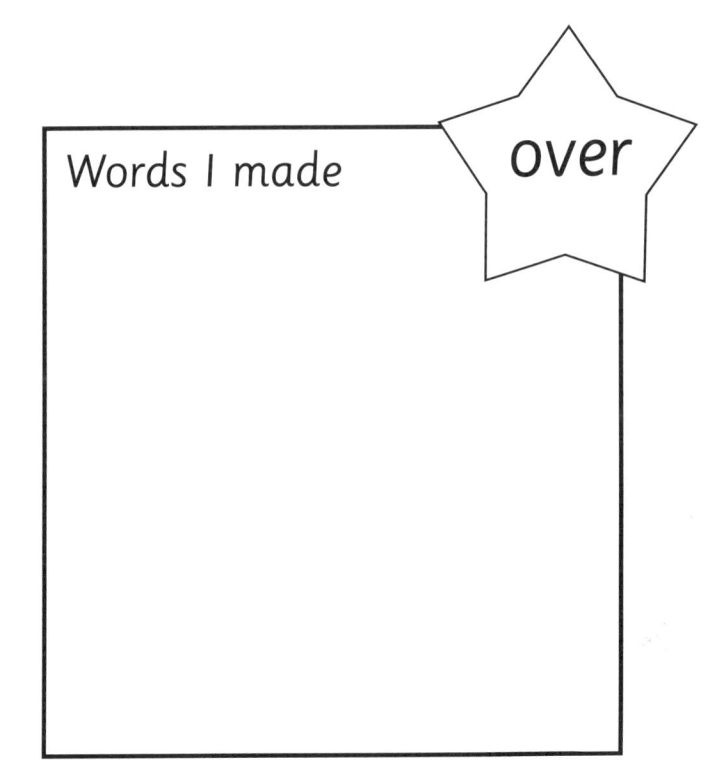

Words I made   over

Name _____ | u-e | UNIT 9
Copymaster 60

Write and say these **u-e** words.

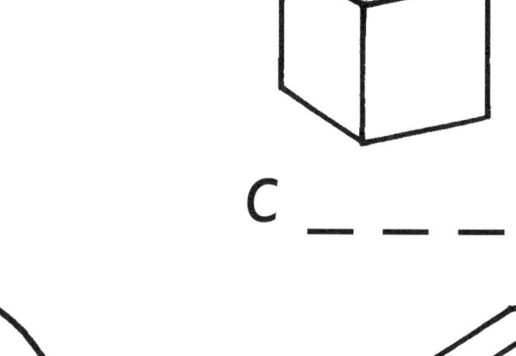

fl _ _ _

c _ _ _

m _ _ _

u-e

t _ _ _

t _ _ _

sal _ _ _

Blend these letters to make words.

m   b
fl   l
   u   e
c   n
t   t

Words I made

over

Name _____

Learning map 9 UNIT 9
Copymaster 61

Write three star words. [ ] [ ] [ ]

Write the words.

_ _ _ _	_ _ _ _	_ _ _ _	_ _ _ _

Match the pairs.

cage   bike
June   hose
like   page
close   tune

Write four more words for each sound.

a-e	
i-e	
o-e	
u-e	

Name _____ ai UNIT 10
Copymaster 62

Write and say these **ai** words.

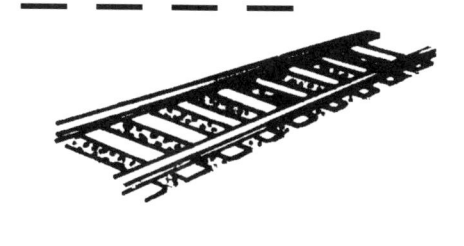

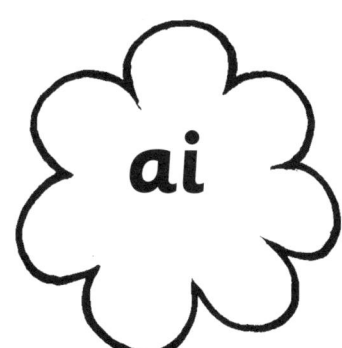

_ _ _ _

_ _ _ _

_ _ _ _

_ _ _ _

_ _ _ _

_ _ _ ry

Blend these letters to make words.

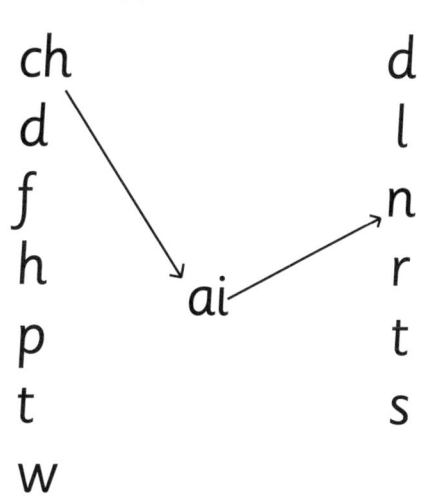

ch
d
f
h   ai
p
t
w

d
l
n
r
t
s

y

Words I made

chain

eight

Name _____ |ay| UNIT 10
Copymaster 63

Write and say these **ay** words.

_ _ _

_ _ _ _

_ _ _

j _ _

_ _ _ _

eight

Add **day** to each one.

Mon
Tues
Wednes
Thurs   day
Fri
Satur
Sun

The days of the week

Name _____   oi   UNIT 10
Copymaster 64

Write and say these **oi** words.

p _ _ _ _

_ _ _ _   b _ _ _

n _ _ se

cub _ _ _

Blend these letters to make words.

b   l
c   oi   n
           ns
j
           nt

Words I made   half

Name _____

oy

UNIT 10
Copymaster 65

Make words with the word wheel.

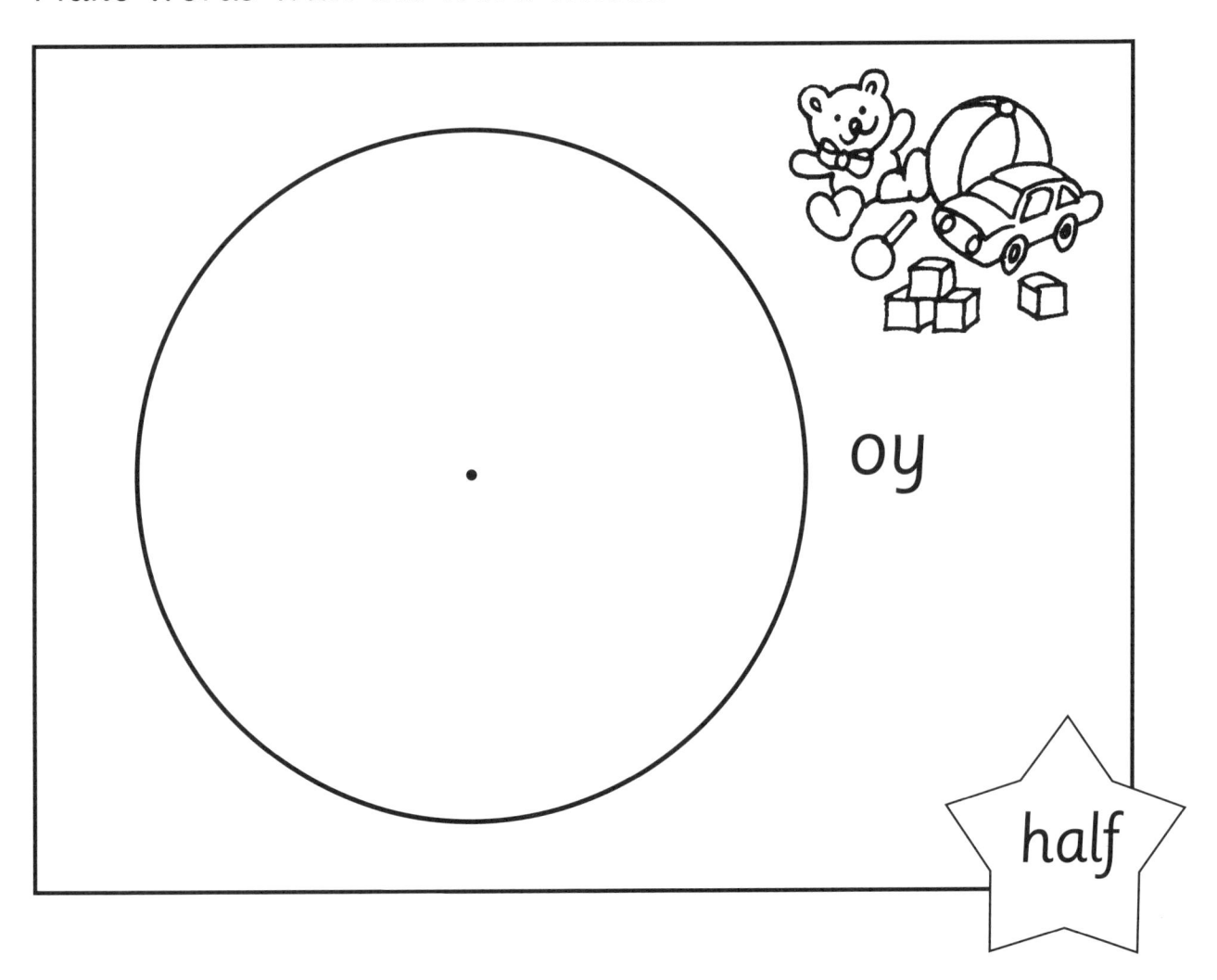

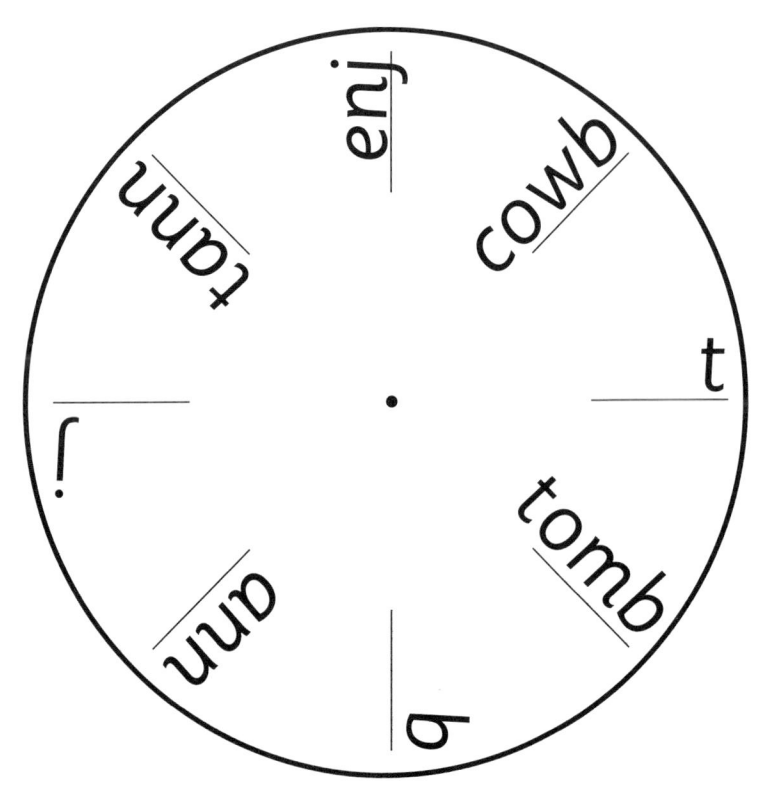

oy

half

Words I made

Name _____

ee | UNIT 10
Copymaster 66

Write and say these **ee** words.

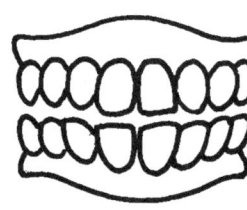

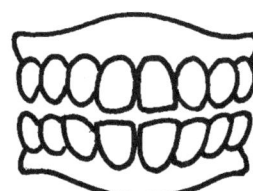

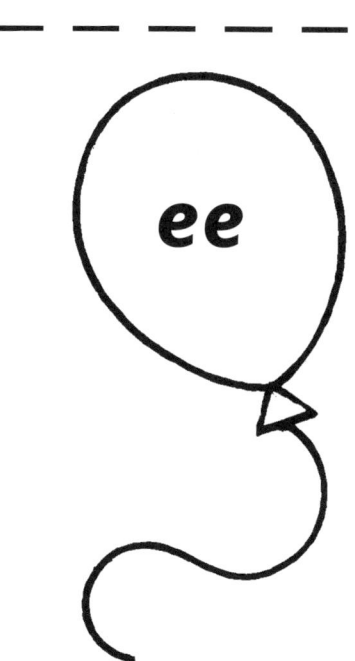

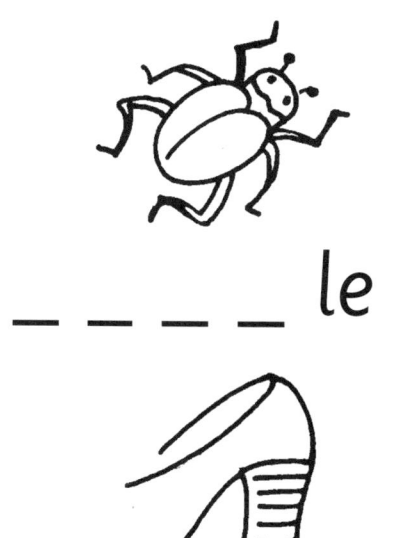

Blend these letters to make words.

b
f
h   ee
k
s
t

d
f
l
p
n
th

Words I made

when

Name _____ |ea| UNIT 10
Copymaster 67

Write and say these **ea** words.

_ _ _ _   _ _ _ _

ea

_ _ _ _

_ _ _ _   _ _ _ _   _ _ _

Fill the wall with **ea** words.

when

Name _____

Make words with the word wheel.

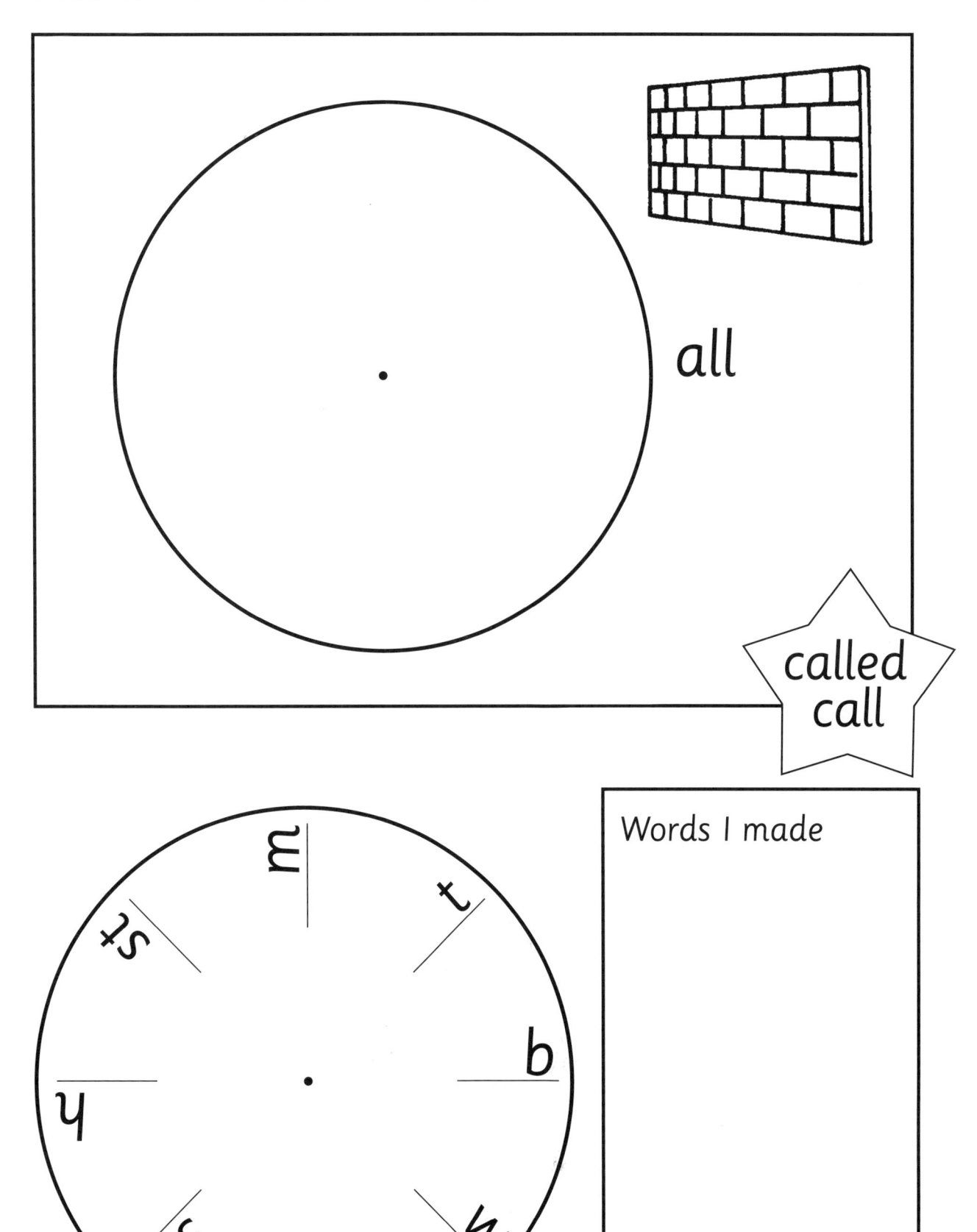

all

UNIT 10
Copymaster 68

all

called
call

Words I made

Name _____

Learning map 10 UNIT 10
Copymaster 69

Write five star words.

Colour in the long vowel sounds.

snail, ball, bent, boy, met, been, spoil, spill, bolt, say, snatch, meat

Write three words for each sound.

ai	ay	oi
oy	ee	ea

Name _____

| oo | UNIT 11
Copymaster 70 |

Make **oo** words.

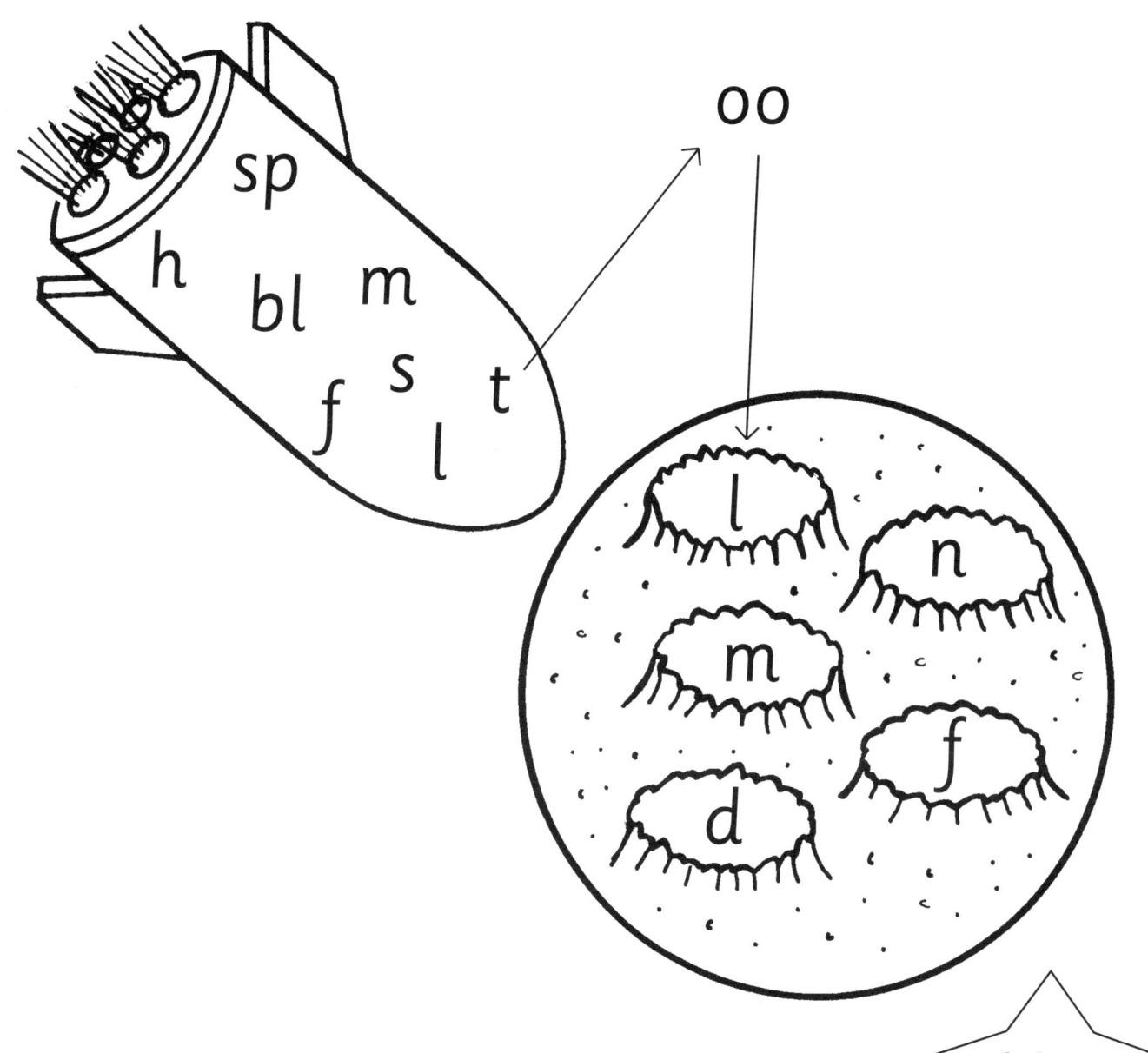

oo

sp, h, bl, m, s, t, f, l

l, n, m, f, d

Find **oo** words.

oson	
phoo	
moro	
sonop	
fodo	
ohfo	

Words I made
loom

blue

Name _____

Write and say these oo words.

oo	book _ _ _ _	hook _ _ _ _
foot _ _ _ _	br _ _ _	sh _ _ _
_ _ _ _ er	s _ _ _	l _ _ _

oo   UNIT 11
Copymaster 71

Blend these letters to make words.

l
h ⟶ oo
c   r ⟶ k
f
b

t

Words I made
hook

who

Name _____ oa   UNIT 11
Copymaster 72

Write and say these **oa** words.

Word search

t	o	a	s	t	e	r
o	c	r	o	a	k	o
a	p	o	a	c	h	a
d	e	e	p	i	n	d
l	o	a	d	e	d	s
c	o	a	c	h	e	s

Words I found

who

Name _____　　　　　　ou　　UNIT 11
Copymaster 73

Write and say these **ou** words.

ou	 m _ _ _ _ _ (mouth)	 h _ _ _ _ (house)
c _ _ _ _ _ (couch)	_ _ _ _ _ (pound)	s _ _ _ _ (spout/snout)
tr _ _ _ (trout)	_ _ _ _ _ (mouse)	h _ _ nd (hound)

Blend these letters to make words.

b　　　　　　nd
f
h　　　ou　　nt
m
p　　　　　　se
r
s　　　　　　t

Words I made

★ house

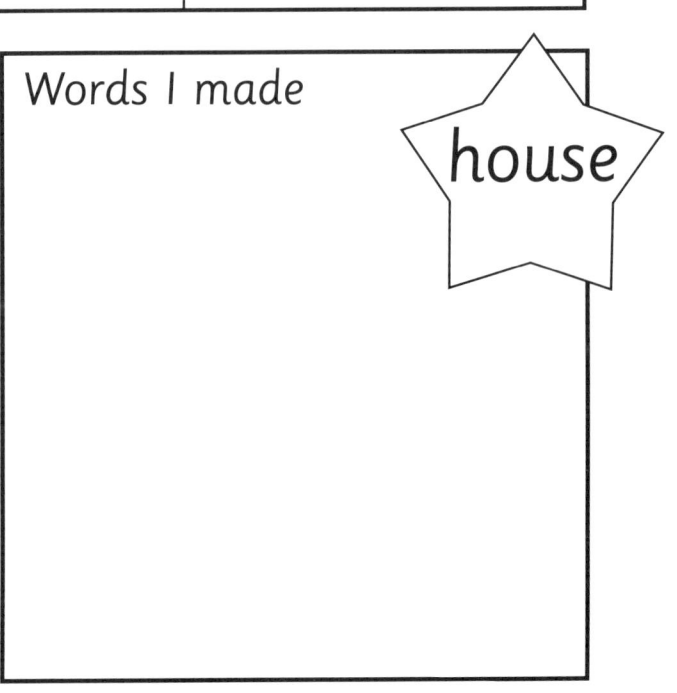

Name _____

aw   UNIT 11
Copymaster 74

Write and say these **aw** words.

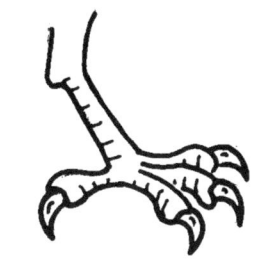

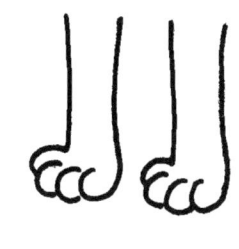

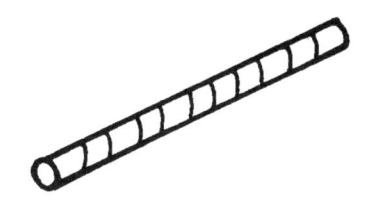

_ _ _

p _ _ _

y _ _ _

cr _ _ _

aw

_ _ _ _

_ _ _ _

Word search

s	t	r	a	w	d	s
h	a	w	k	s	r	h
a	f	a	w	n	a	a
w	c	l	a	w	w	w
l	j	a	w	a	e	l
c	r	a	w	l	r	s

Words I found

own

Name _____ | ew | UNIT 11
Copymaster 75

Write and say these **ew** words.

ch _ _

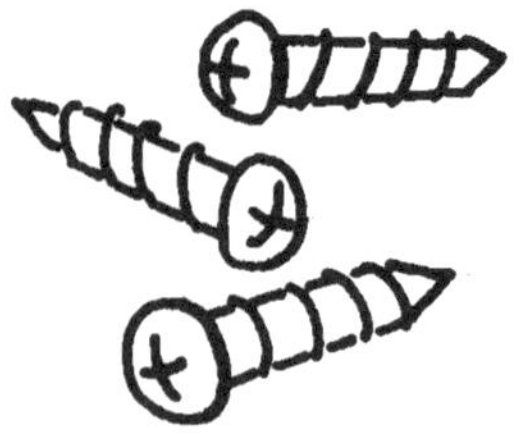

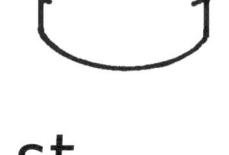

st _ _

_ _ _ _ _

ew

y _ _

n _ _ _

dr _ _

Match these letters to make words.

br
cr
dr
f   +   ew
gr
n
shr
st

Words I made

laugh

Name _____ `ow`   UNIT 11
Copymaster 76

Make and write these **ow** words.

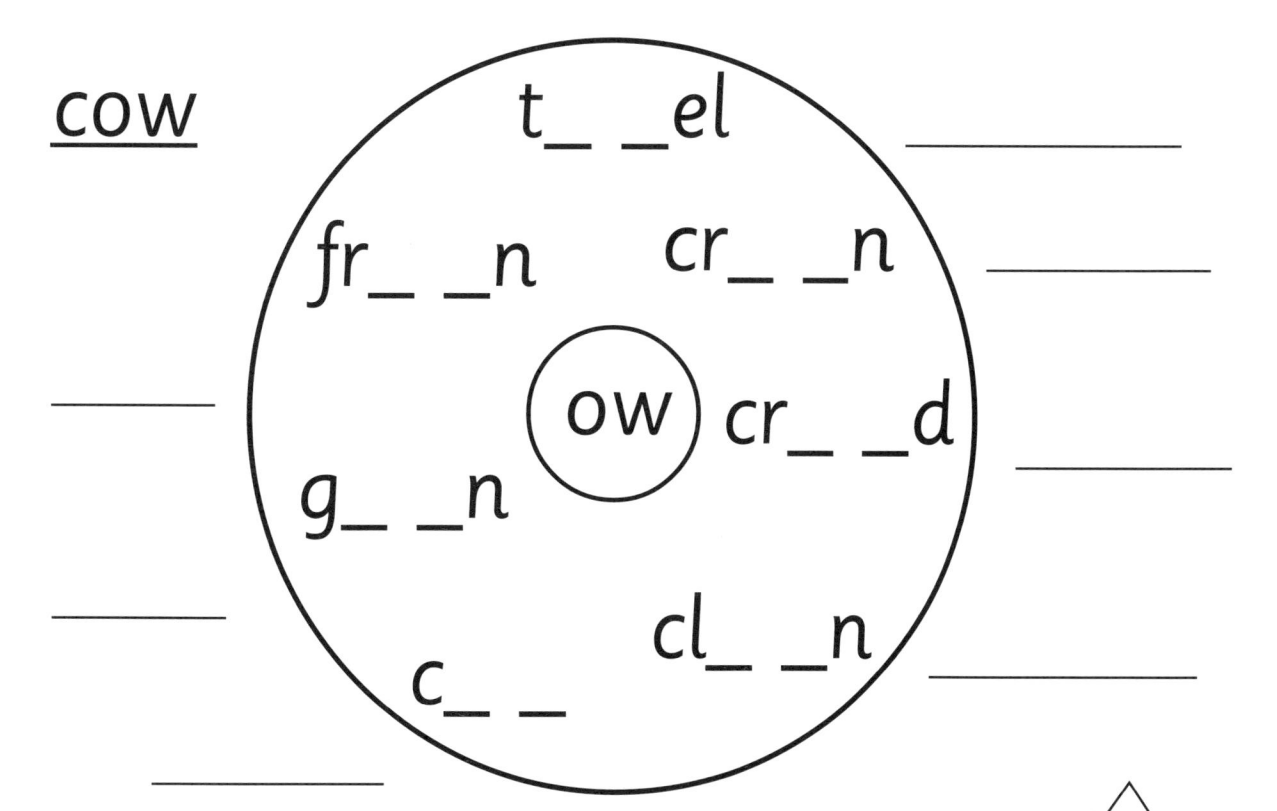

cow

t_ _el

fr_ _n   cr_ _n

ow   cr_ _d

g_ _n

c_ _   cl_ _n

★ laugh

Fill the wall with **ow** words.

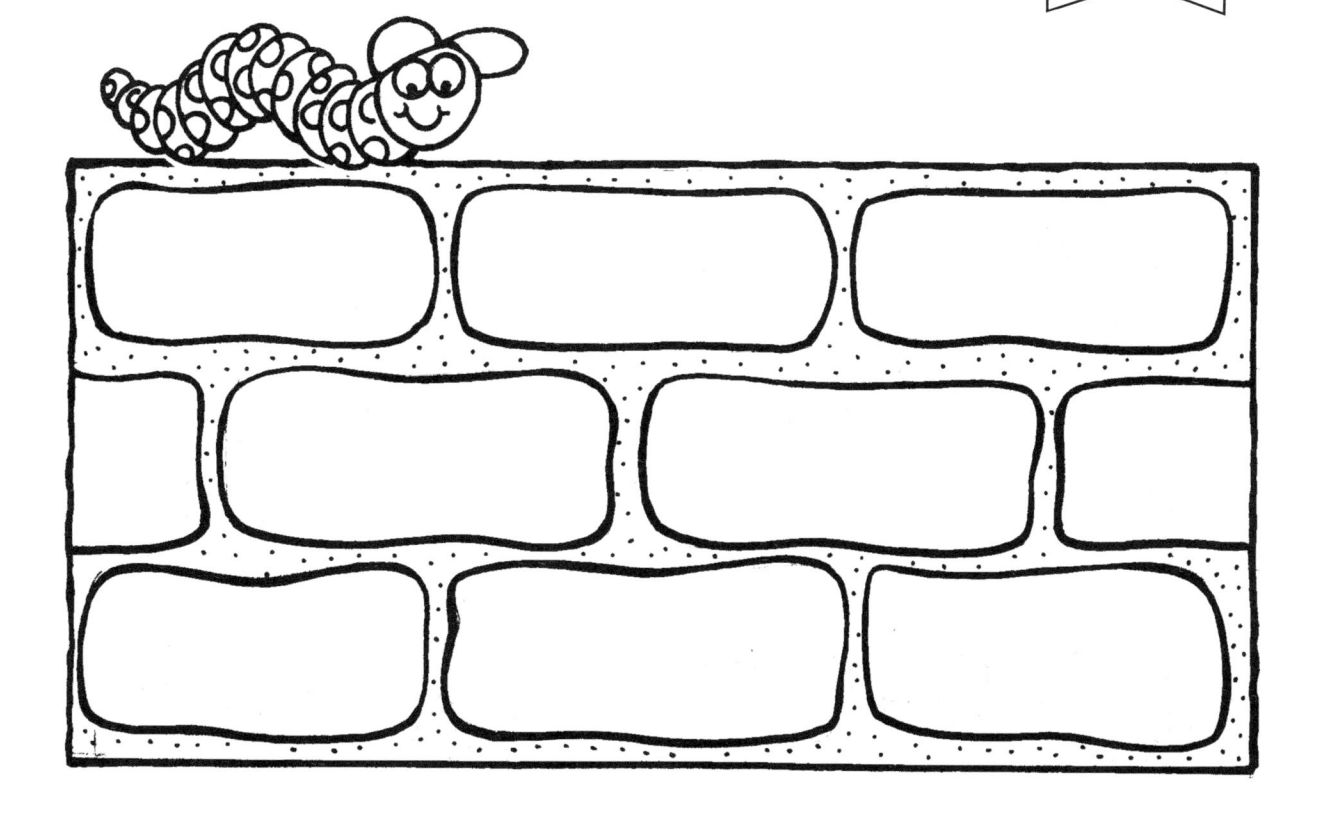

Name _____

Learning map 11 UNIT 11
Copymaster 77

Write five star words.

Write words for each sound.

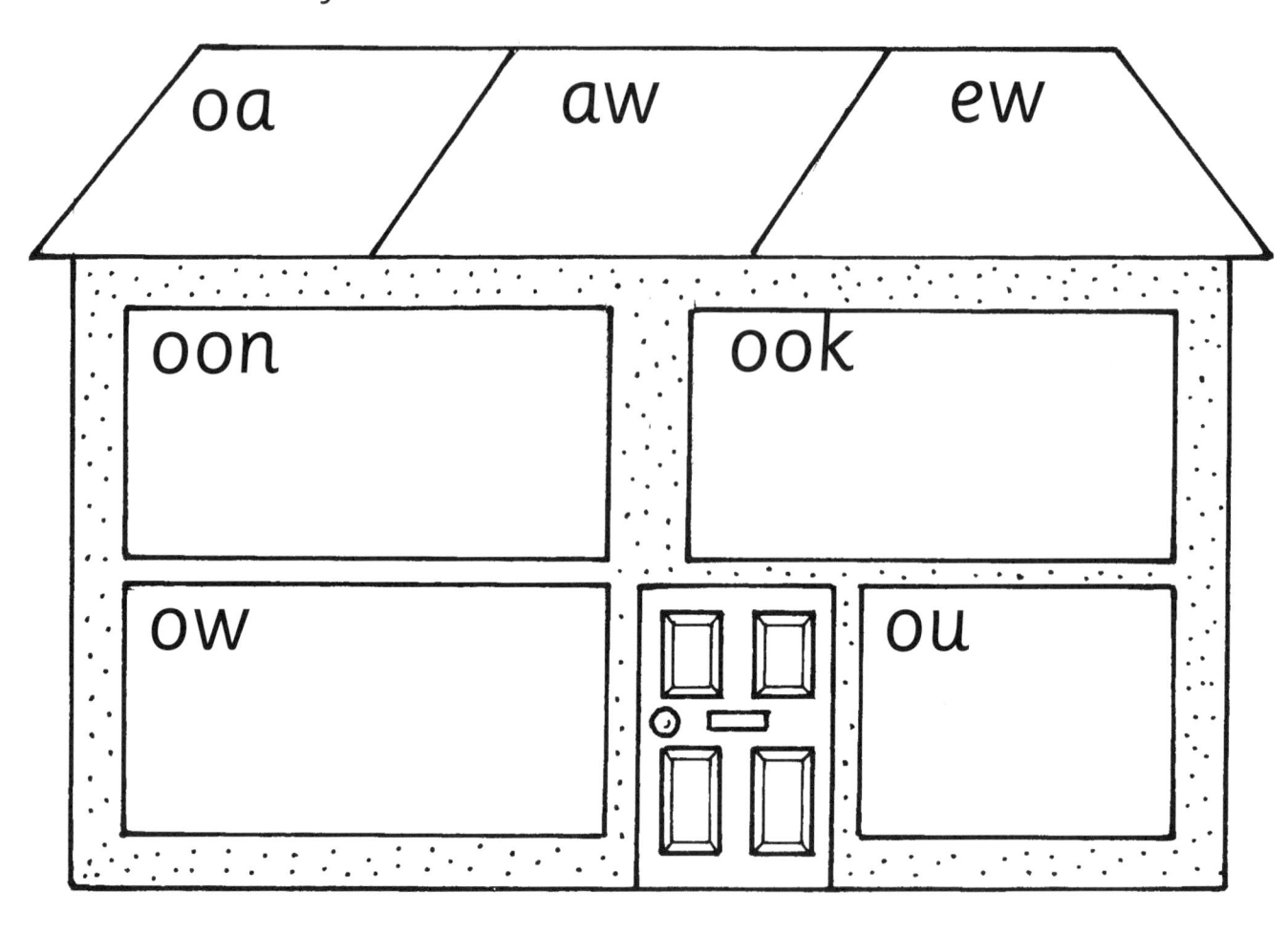

oa / aw / ew

oon

ook

ow

ou

Match each picture to its long vowel sound.

oo   oi
all   ou
      ai   ow
  oa
              ea
      ee

Name _____ | ar | UNIT 12
Copymaster 78

Write and say these **ar** words.

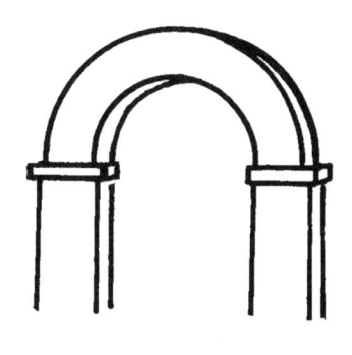

Match these beginnings and endings.

bar — cel
car —→ den
gar — ket
lar — pet
mar — der
par — ber

Words I made

carpet

where

Name _____   **are**   UNIT 12
Copymaster 79

Add **are** and say the words.

c _ _ _   st _ _ _

      sc _ _ _   gl _ _ _

d _ _ _   **are**

      f _ _ _   fl _ _ _

b _ _ _   h _ _ _

Match these beginnings with this ending.

bl
c
d
fl
h
sh
squ

are

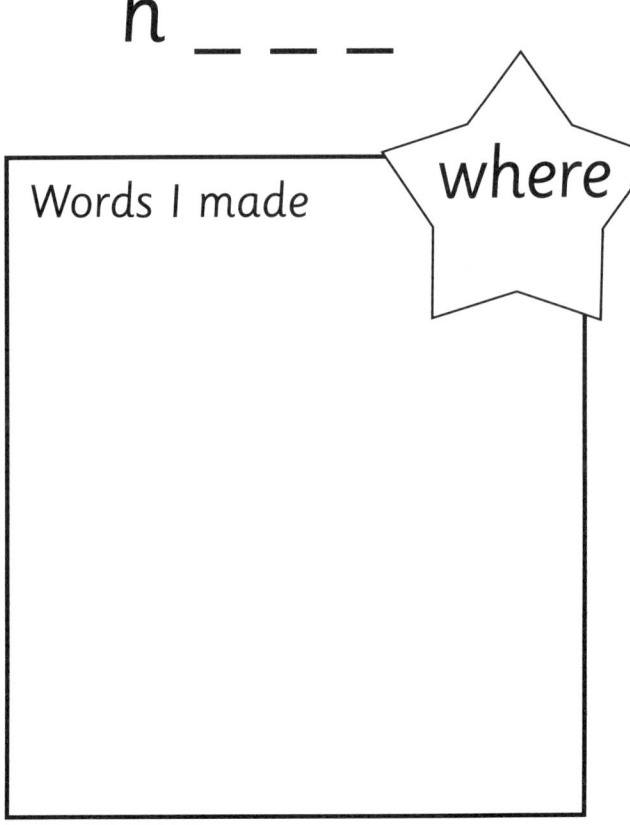

Words I made

where

Name _____   air   UNIT 12
Copymaster 80

Write and say these **air** words.

p _ _ _

_ _ _ _ y

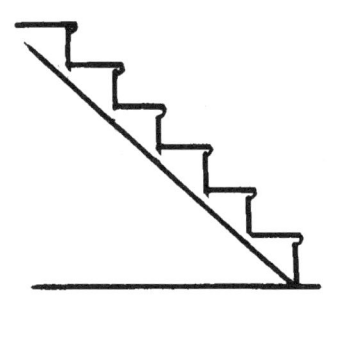

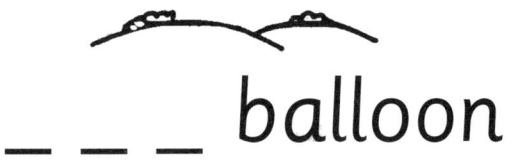

_ _ _ balloon

Blend these letters to make words.

p
h   y
fl   air
f   s
d

Words I made

what

Name _____ | er | UNIT 12
Copymaster 81

Write and say these **er** words.

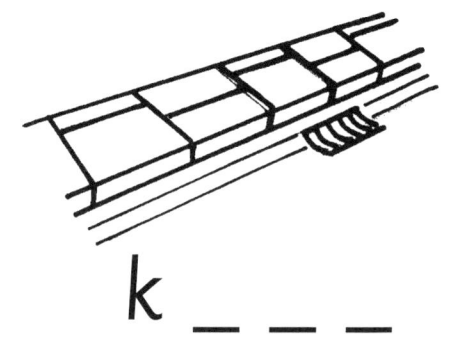

f _ _ _ _   h _ _ b   k _ _ _

g _ _ bil   s _ _ pent   what

Match the beginnings with the endings.

Short vowel sounds	Words I made
copp	
dinn	
filt + er	
fing	
hamm	
scann	

Long vowel sounds	Words I made
bak	
div	
fiv + er	
dri	
jok	
tig	

Name _____ | ear | UNIT 12
Copymaster 82

Make and write these **ear** words.

year

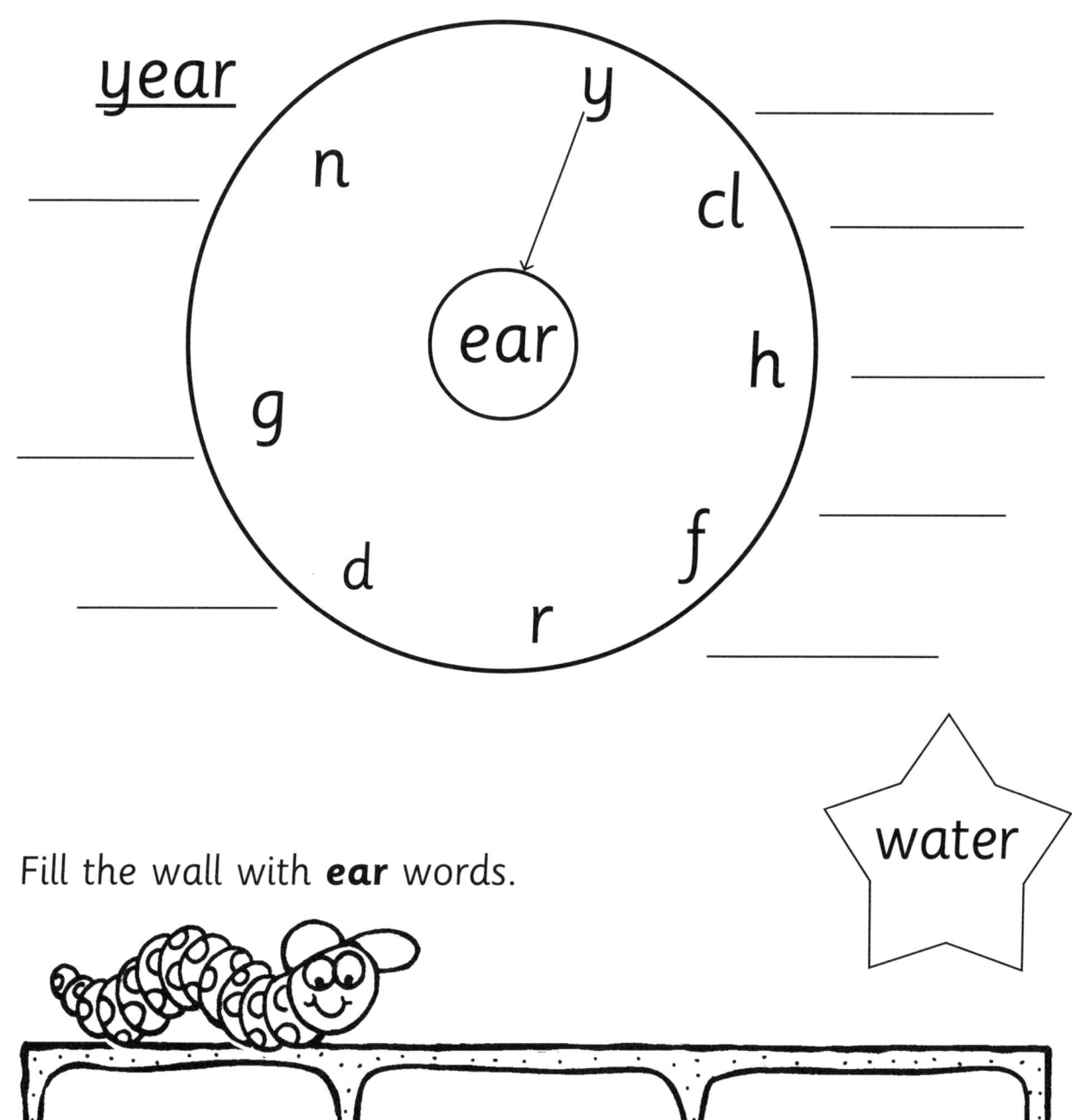

- n
- y
- cl
- g
- h
- d
- f
- r

(ear)

Fill the wall with **ear** words.

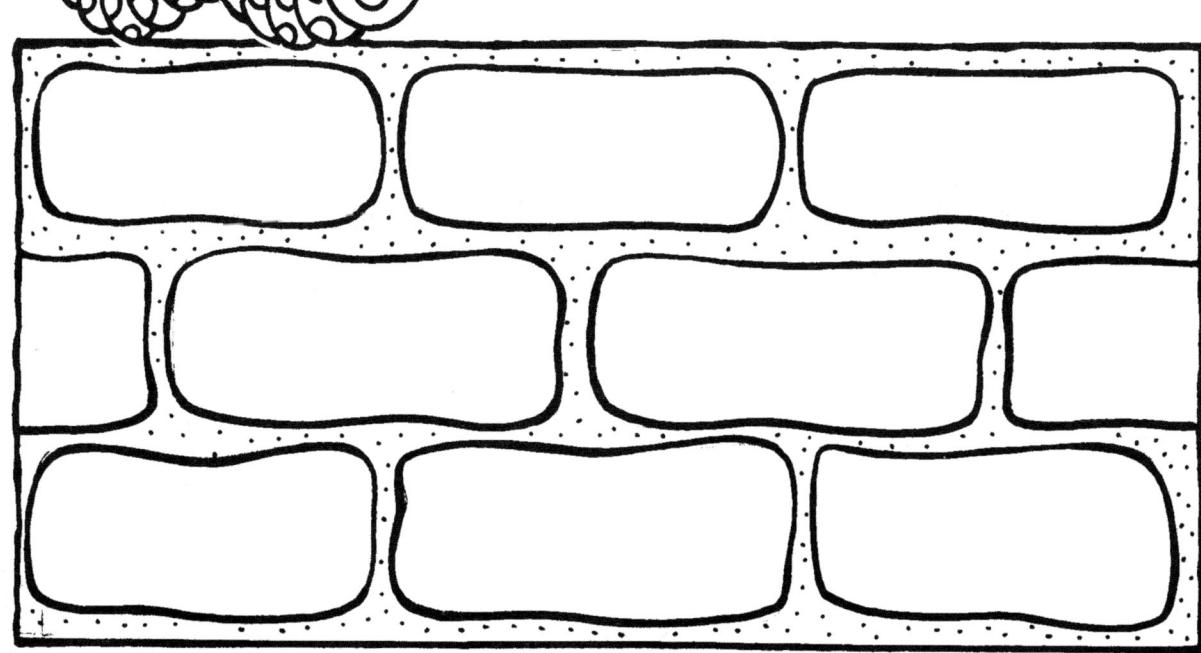

water

Name _____

eer UNIT 12
Copymaster 83

Make and write **eer** words.

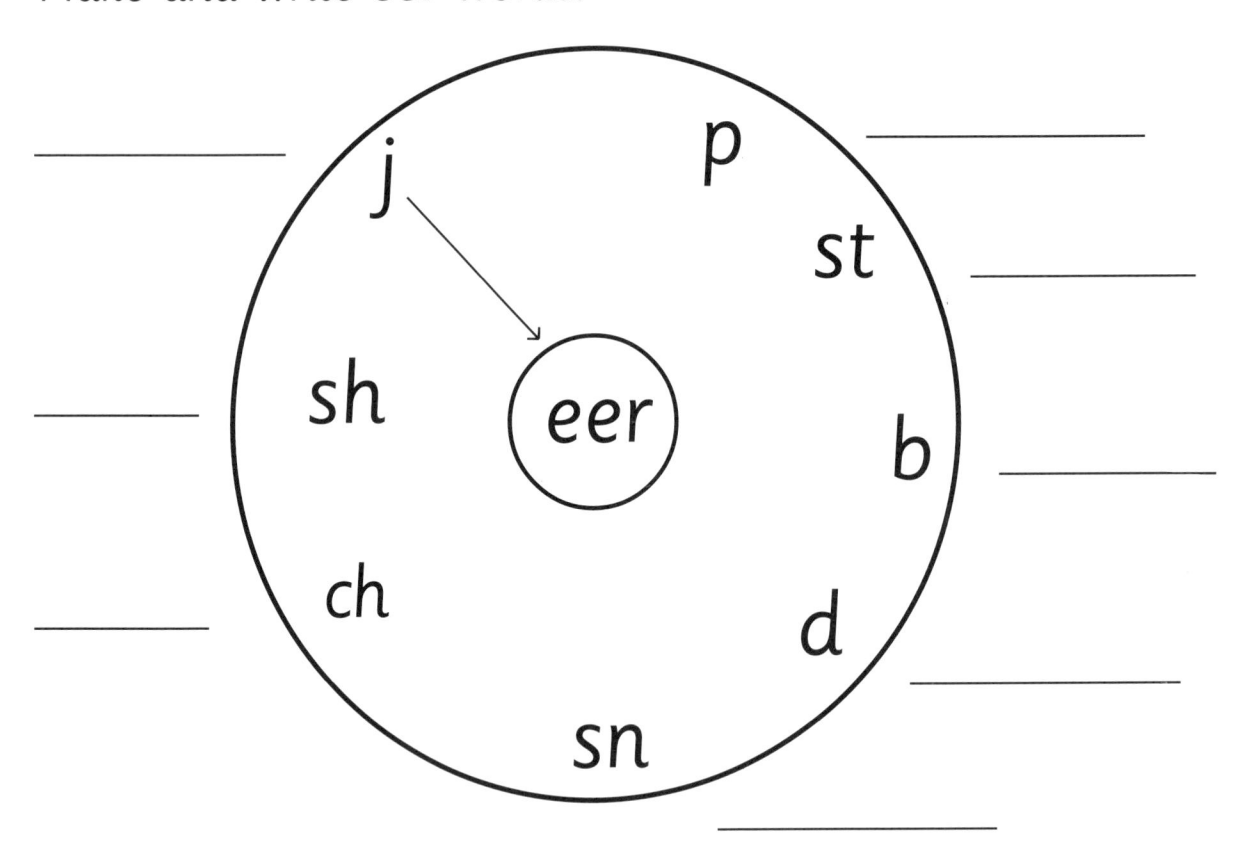

(wheel with **eer** in center; surrounding letters: j, p, st, b, d, sn, ch, sh)

Word search

s	h	e	e	r	j
n	e	e	d	o	e
e	b	e	e	r	e
e	s	t	e	e	r
r	o	a	r	e	d
c	a	r	e	e	r

Words I found

water

Name _____ Learning map 12   UNIT 12
Copymaster 84

Write five star words.

Match the pairs.

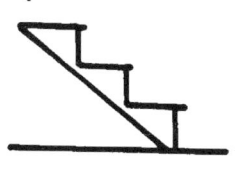

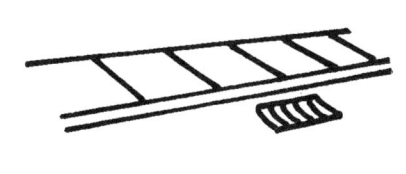

_ _ _ _ _ _

k _ _ b

_ _ _ _ _ _

h _ _ _

t _ _ _ _

_ _ _ _

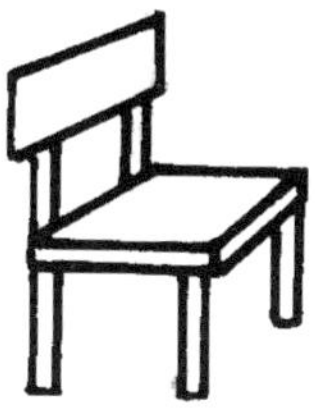

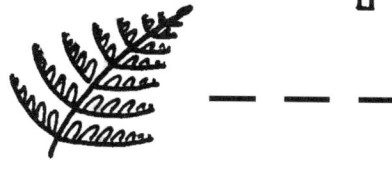

f _ _ _ _

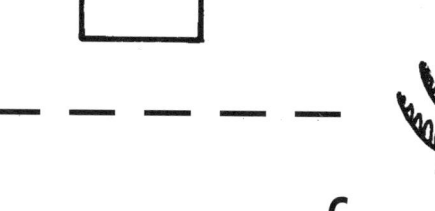

Find three more words for each blend.

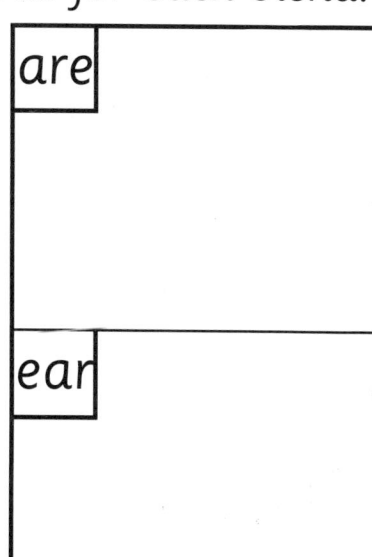

ar		are		air	
er		ear		eer	

Name _____

| ir |

UNIT 13
Copymaster 85

Write and say these **ir** words.

_ _ _ _

_ _ _ _

f _ _ st

_ _ _

_ _ _

Blend these letters to make words.

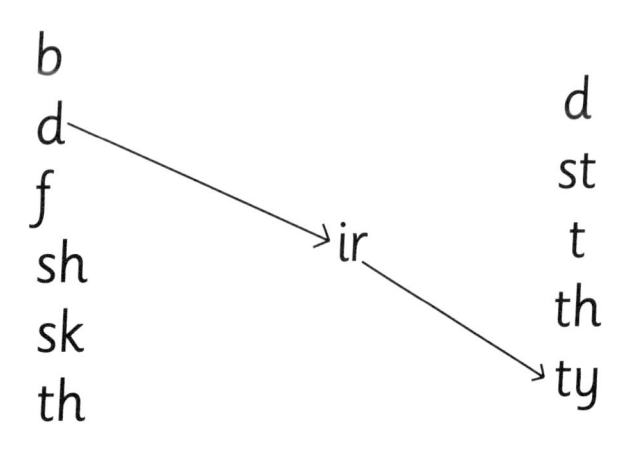

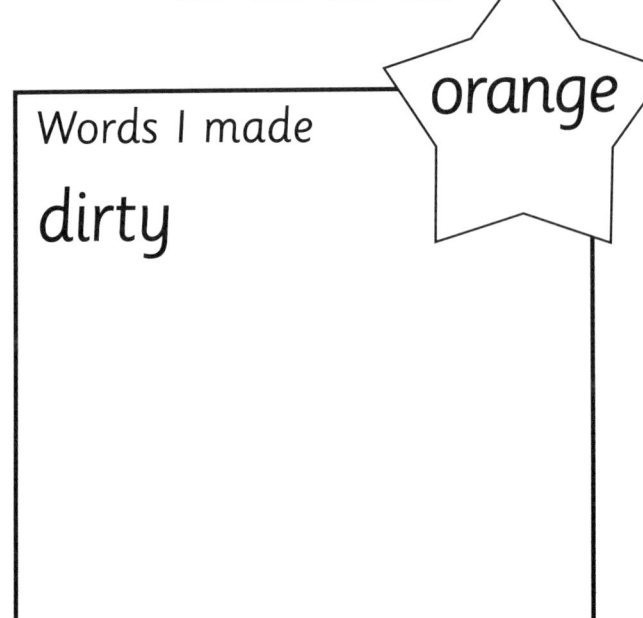

b
d
f
sh
sk
th

→ ir

d
st
t
th
ty

Words I made

dirty

orange

Name _____   ire   UNIT 13
Copymaster 86

Make words with the word wheel.

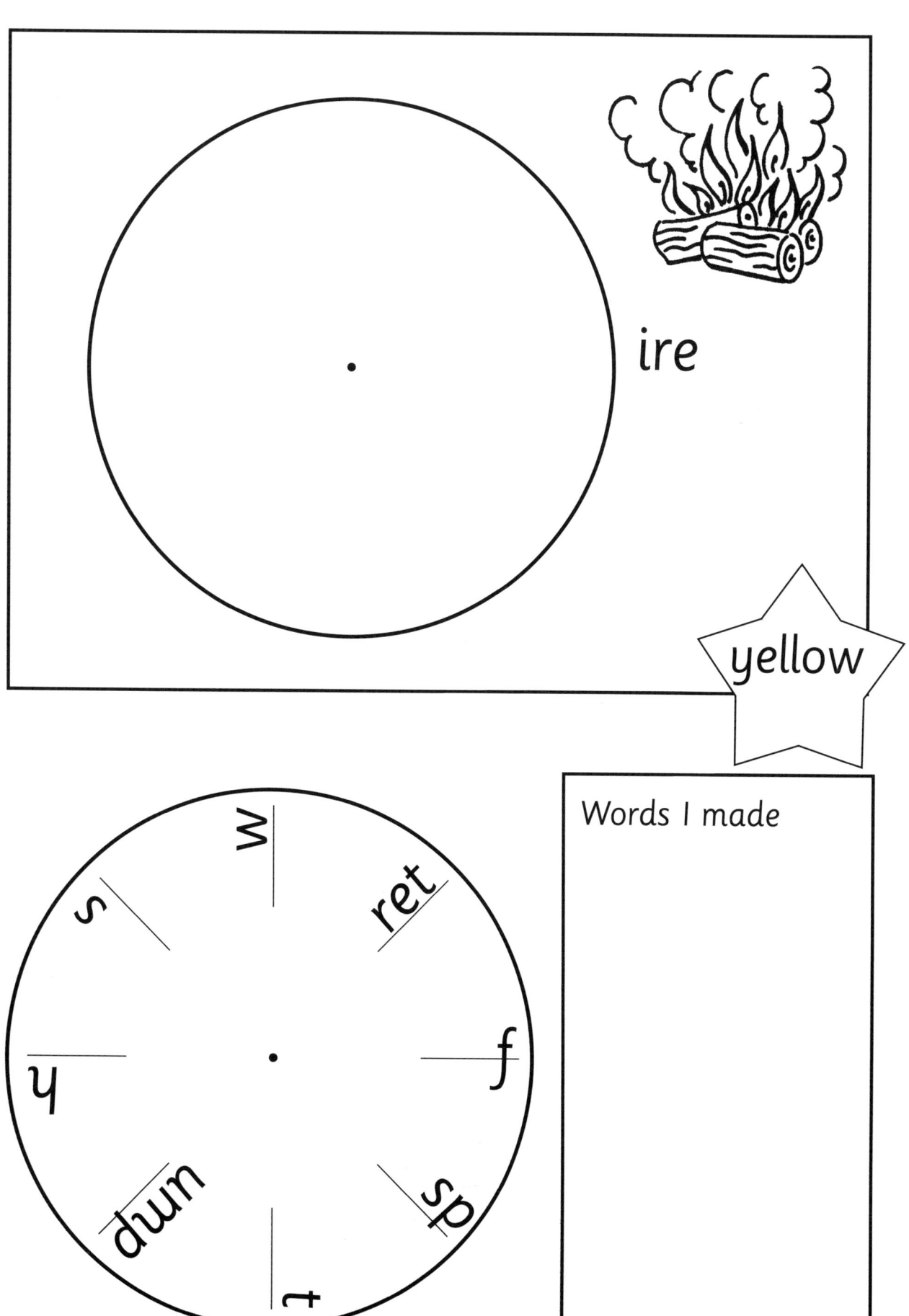

yellow

Words I made

Name _____ | or | UNIT 13
Copymaster 87

Make and write **or** words.

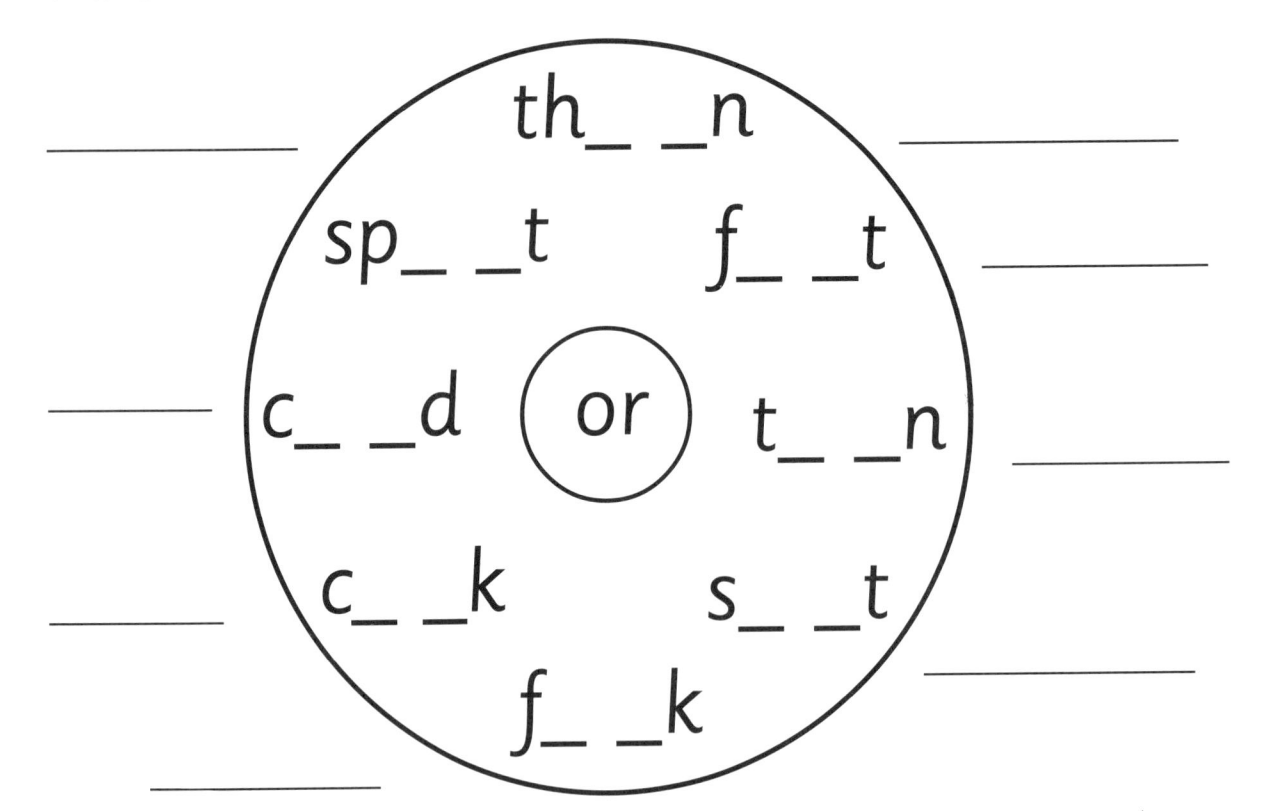

th_ _n

sp_ _t   f_ _t

c_ _d   (or)   t_ _n

c_ _k   s_ _t

f_ _k

door

Fill the wall with **or** words.

Name _____

ore

UNIT 13
Copymaster 88

Write and say these **ore** words.

_ _ _ _

_ _ _ _ _

ore

_ _ _ _

st _ _ _

Add these beginnings to this ending.

b
c
m
s   +   ore
sh
st
w

Words I made

door

Name _____

ur | UNIT 13
Copymaster 89

Write and say these **ur** words.

b _ _ _

_ _ _ _ e

_ _ _ _ _ ey

_ _ _ _ e

_ _ _ _ le

ur

Word search

t	u	r	f	o	s	t
u	c	p	u	r	l	u
r	h	u	r	t	u	r
n	u	r	l	u	r	k
i	r	p	b	r	p	e
p	c	l	u	p	u	y
a	h	e	r	s	b	s

Words I found

school

Name _____ |ure| UNIT 13
Copymaster 90

Make words with the word wheel.

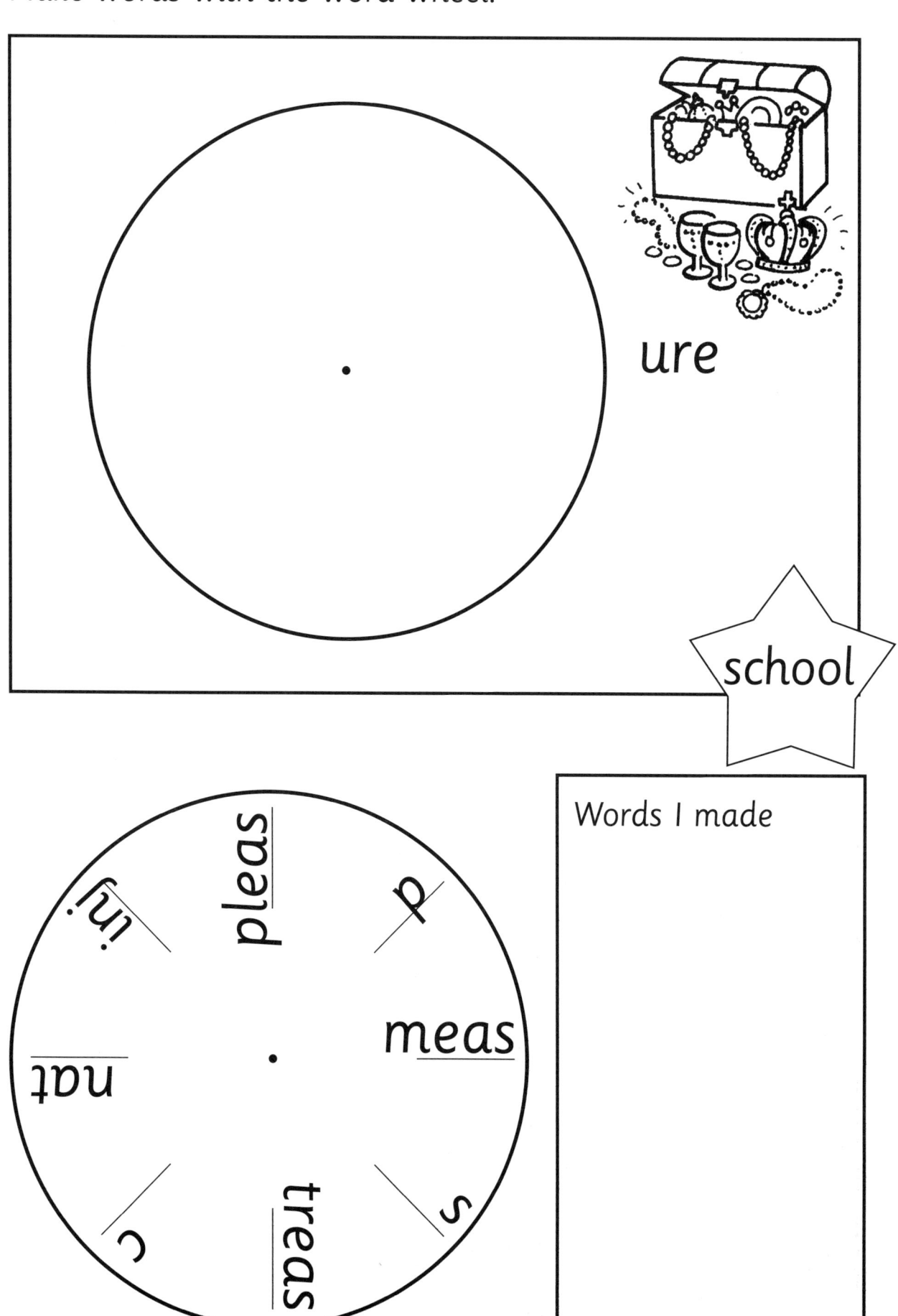

ure

school

Words I made

pleas
p
inj
meas
nat
c
s
treas

Name _____

Learning map 13 — UNIT 13
Copymaster 91

Write five star words.

Write two more words for each blend.

ir	or	ur

ire	ore	ure

Match the pairs.

skirt — shirt
spire — shore
fort — sure
core — short
lure — shire
spur — fur

Find a word in each word.

secure — **cure**
fortunate — _____
further — _____
encore — _____
inspire — _____
dirtiness — _____

High frequency words

about	after	again
an	another	as
back	ball	be
because	bed	been
boy	brother	but
by	call	called
came	can't	could
did	do	don't
dig	door	down
first	from	girl
good	got	had

High frequency words

half	has	have
help	her	here
him	his	home
house	how	if
jump	just	last
laugh	little	live
lived	love	made
make	man	many
may	more	much
must	name	new
next	night	not

High frequency words

now	off	old
once	one	or
our	out	over
people	push	pull
put	ran	saw
school	seen	should
sister	so	some
take	than	that
their	them	then
there	these	three
time	too	took

High frequency words

Copymaster 95

tree	two	us
very	want	water
way	were	what
when	where	who
will	with	would
your		

Alphabet cards

Copymaster 96

a	b	c
d	e	f
g	h	i
j	k	l
m	n	o

Alphabet cards

Copymaster 97

p	qu	r
s	t	u
v	w	x
y	z	ff
ll	ss	er

High Frequency Words Check List: Years 1 and 2   Pupil's Name_____

about			him			put		
after			his			ran		
again			home			saw		
an			house			school		
another			how			seen		
as			if			should		
back			jump			sister		
ball			just			so		
be			last			some		
because			laugh			take		
bed			little			than		
been			live(d)			that		
boy			love			their		
brother			made			them		
but			make			then		
by			man			there		
call(ed)			many			these		
came			may			three		
can't			more			time		
could			much			too		
did			must			took		
do			name			tree		
don't			new			two		
dig			next			us		
door			night			very		
down			not			want		
first			now			water		
from			off			way		
girl			old			were		
good			once			what		
got			one			when		
had			or			where		
half			our			who		
has			out			with		
have			over			will		
help			people			would		
her			pull			your		
here			push					

Scores

List 1	Date	No. of errors
Tested		
Checked		
Checked		

List 2	Date	No. of errors
Tested		
Checked		
Checked		

List 3	Date	No. of errors
Tested		
Checked		
Checked		

My star words book

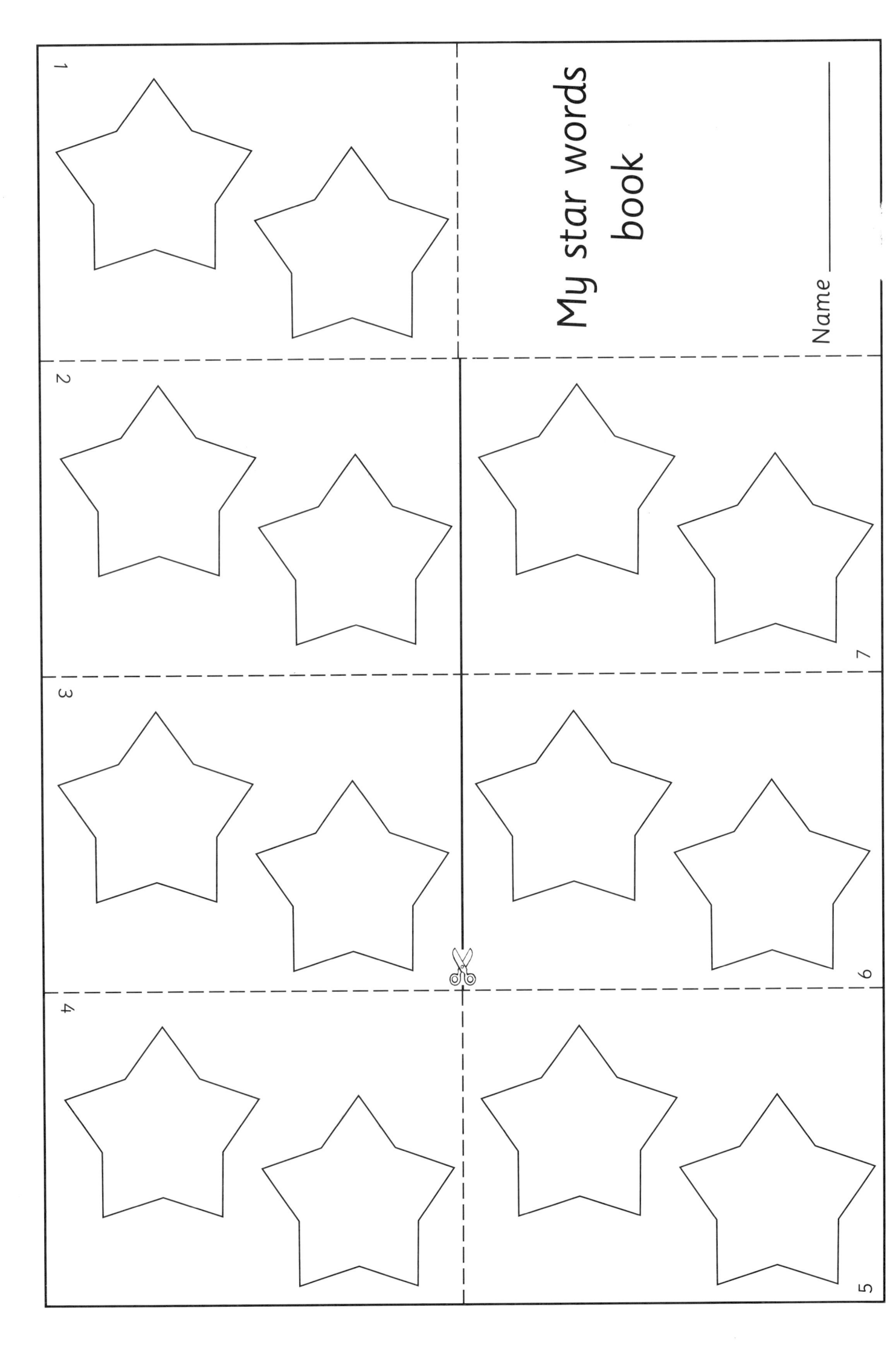

Name _____